Poker books from D&B

Poker 24/7
by Stewart Reuben
1-904468-16-0, 256pp, $24.95 / £15.99

Poker on the Internet
by Andrew Kinsman
1-904468-20-9, 208pp, $19.95 / £12.99

Beginners Guide to Limit Hold'em
by Byron Jacobs
1-904468-21-7, 208pp, $19.95 / £12.99

How Good is Your Limit Hold 'em?
by Byron Jacobs with Jim Brier
1-904468-15-2, 192pp, $19.95 / £12.99

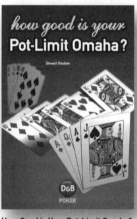

How Good is Your Pot-Limit Omaha?
by Stewart Reuben,
1-904468-07-1, 192pp, $19.95 / £12.99

How Good is Your Pot-Limit Hold'em?
by Stewart Reuben
1-904468-08- ... `19.95 / £12.99

Hold'em on the Come
by Rolf Slotboom and Drew Mason
1-904468-23-3, 272pp, $19.95 / £12.99

D&B POKER
www.dandbpoker.com
info@dandbpublishing.com

Princes of Darkness

THE WORLD OF HIGH STAKES BLACKJACK

 Carl Sampson

First published in 2006 by D&B Publishing

Copyright © 2006 Carl Sampson

British Library Cataloguing-in-Publication Data
A catalogue record for this book is available from the British Library.

ISBN 1-904468-34-9
ISBN 13 987-1-904468-34-9

All sales enquiries should be directed to:
D & B Publishing, PO Box 18, Hassocks,
West Sussex BN6 9WR, UK

Tel: +44 (0)1273 834680, Fax: +44 (0)1273 831629,
e-mail: info@dandbpublishing.com,
Website: www.dandbpublishing.com
Carl Sampson can be contacted at Carl@Pokerquest.f9.co.uk

Cover design by Horatio Monteverde.
Production by Navigator Guides.
Printed and bound in the US by Versa Press.

CONTENTS

Introduction 7

1 A Breath of Fresh Air 13
2 Where's that Business Card? 22
3 Blackjack 101 33
4 Getting Down to Business 42
5 The Theory of Shuffle Tracking 65
6 The Second Meeting 78
7 The Man with the Plan 87
8 Keeping up the Standards 103
9 Merry Christmas, Mr Sampson 114
10 Onward Christian Soldiers 137
11 D-day – in more ways than One 151
12 Russian Roulette: it's the only Game in Town 160
13 That was the Week that was 168
14 So, just what is going on? 191
15 Black Birthday 197
16 The End of the Beginning 204

INTRODUCTION

This is more than just your run of the mill blackjack theory book. It is also more than just the story of my obsession with hitting back at an industry that constantly irritated me for one reason or another. Nor is it simply about revenge for promotions denied me not once but several times throughout the years while I was employed as a croupier. *Princes of Darkness* is in fact the remarkable story of a team of successful high stakes advantage players that took the casino industry for a seven figure sum from 1998 through to 2002.

It is also a window into the world of the gaming industry, seen through the eyes of someone who has operated from both sides of the fence. The characters are real people and the events described in this book actually happened. However, I have changed the identities of the members of the team who I once dubbed "the four musketeers", and kept secret the names of the casinos where these events took place. I have also slightly altered the dates when these events actually happened for reasons that I do not want to go into.

I would like to express my sincere thanks to all the people that made this venture possible, which I have not yet done adequately. Without the help of "John", "Kevin" and "Patty", this book wouldn't have been possible and would never have been published. But my greatest thanks are reserved for "Steve", who as the financial backer provided the bankroll to attack the games at a high level. I would also like to thank the numerous "helpers" that we had along the way. You know who you are.

The strategies we used will amaze you. Our success was not achieved merely by simple card counting although card counting did play its part. If we had merely card counted then it is probable that our "career" wouldn't have lasted the time that it did nor would we have won the amount that we did. I implemented a wide array of tactics and camouflage techniques that kept our anonymity for as long as possible.

We hit the casinos with an arsenal of weapons, to which over a four-year period players had no defence. We used psychological play against dealers, shuffle tracking, conventional counting and a wide assortment of other techniques that will almost blow your mind at times. We didn't have a choice as the overall quality of the blackjack games was poor in terms of potential profitability just from ordinary card counting.

This book will also teach players who cannot card count how to do it, although this is not the book's primary purpose. It will also teach the secret and rarely executed art of shuffle tracking, which when done well is a very powerful weapon indeed and can be difficult to spot even for trained counters, because much of the strategy runs contrary to what is typical card counting technique. This book is part manual and part story, which is deliberate as my intention was to make the learning process as interesting and entertaining as possible.

Early days

I first entered the gaming industry in 1989 as a trainee croupier. The money was abysmal but I had a chronic lack of options at the time. My partner and future ex-wife was pregnant and expecting our first child, and I was out of a job. Having basically messed around during my final two years at school, I was rather desperate and had no meaningful qualifications to speak of. During that year I became aware of card counting simply by picking up a book in my local library.

That book was the famous *Beat the Dealer*, by Edward Thorp, which was the first major selling blackjack card counting book of its kind. It was the first serious source of motivation for me, and I went on to read and study almost every worthwhile blackjack book that had ever been written. I practised my card counting skills in live casino conditions while either dealing or supervising the games.

My counting became so fast that I could count down an entire deck in roughly 20 seconds and I could scan seven hands of blackjack with the merest glance at the table. I could easily carry on a conversation with several people at the same time and still not be in danger of losing the count. At that time, I never would have believed that my interest in blackjack would be anything other than purely theoretical, but I did enjoy having knowledge of a game that few others had.

That statement may surprise many American readers, after all card counting has been common knowledge in the United States for some time, and many dealers over there can count very well. But it is different in England, where it is rare to find anyone with skill above and beyond the basic counting method of just adding and subtracting 1, based on certain numerical card values. There was a very funny story back in 1995 that underlines my point.

A player had been suspected of counting for a couple of hours and I was asked to go and supervise the table after coming back from my break. I decided to track the count. Even if he was using a different counting system from me it would still become apparent when he upped his bet. Within minutes I had concluded that the guy couldn't play: his basic strategy (decisions on standing, splitting, hitting and so on) were all over the place and totally wrong. He was just another usual Friday night asshole who thought that he could play. Just at that moment, a gaming manager came and stood behind my shoulder to observe events. He came over just in time to see the guy hit 17 and receive a 4 to make 21. Within minutes the guy was escorted from the building and I was in stitches. Even now this punter will still be on some database of undesirables simply because the managers and staff are incompetent when it comes to spotting advanced blackjack play.

The 1990s

During the spring and summer of 1996 my life entered a very turbulent phase with the break up of my marriage, and I was very low. I had changed employers during the mid 1990s and was now working for a rival casino across the city. During 1997 and early 1998 I learned the techniques and devised the strategies that you will be reading about in this book. What I never realised at the time was that the termination of my marriage would open a door that I never would have believed even existed. I never could have found the time had I still had full-time family commitments, but it's strange sometimes how things work out for you. Work out they did and I never looked back.

Shortly after leaving the gaming industry for good in the summer of 1998 I worked as a financial consultant for about six months, but my heart was never in it – it was a career that simply didn't suit me. In fact I hated every minute of that job, but I had been desperate to leave the gaming industry and move on. Once again, it's funny how things work out because it was while I was on a company induction course in Bournemouth in August 1998 that I became acquainted with "Steve", who was to later become our backer for the entire project.

Maybe I am one lucky person because, throughout my life as a whole, something or someone has always been on hand to help me through times of trouble. Many people never have that kind of fortune, but I suppose many people view the flip side as well, and take the view that people make their own luck and destiny, and fortune has nothing to do with it. Who is right? I don't know.

I believe that the overwhelming message that comes from reading *Princes of Darkness* is that the casinos really cannot defend themselves from imagination and creativity. In the end anything that involves human beings can be overcome. This means security systems and casino games because they were invented by humans, after all.

I have to admit that I made numerous mistakes during the formulation of my first team. I knew the theory of how to beat the game of blackjack and beat it badly, but I had no experience of building a professional team and keeping them together at that time. The entire series of events seemed to go very quickly and at times it became easy just to be swept along with the sheer momentum of it.

Looking back I think that I did very well, and achieved exceptional results. But we were rough around the edges at the beginning and the enterprise was a massive learning curve for all of us. I think that this is because it is simply not possible to plan for every potential occurrence. My second team operated in a more professional manner than this one but it had a very short life and didn't earn anywhere near as much money.

Since 2002

My association with blackjack stopped in 2002 and I have mainly been playing poker professionally online ever since. A friend of mine even now still makes a good living beating blackjack games with shuffling machines. Don't tell me that you think that it cannot be done, because card counting knowledge is use-less in these games. Whoever mentioned that they were card counting, remember what I have just told you – imagination and creativity.

I know that my friend wins games year in and year out be-cause I trained him. Couple this with the fact that the casinos think that the games cannot be beaten at all and you have the makings of a very good opportunity: these games still have hu-man dealers and supervisors.

So please remember every time you pick this book up that you are about to read about real people and real life events and not something that is make believe on a TV programme with actors. Different people will take various things from this book; most will simply read it for entertainment. But I would take great pleasure if my book provided the inspiration for someone to emulate or surpass what we did and really stick it up them one more time.

Carl "The Dean" Sampson
Sheffield, August 2006

Chapter 1

A Breath of Fresh Air

July 31st 1998

"Last three spins of the evening ladies and gents." Of course everyone around American roulette 1 and 2 were far from fitting that kind of description but this was my last shift in the gaming industry and I was happy. These would be my last few glimpses of the pathetic losers who lie, cheat, blow their wages, verbally abuse staff and basically don't have a life...at least from this side of the table.

Do all punters fit this category? Absolutely not but chances are that anyone who is sad enough still to be around at 3.50am probably does. I couldn't believe that I was finally getting out of this crappy industry. I knew people who had done well for themselves in this job, seen the world and got paid properly for it, but it is a million miles from that in this gloomy city, in a gaming sense anyway. Despite all this, was there really a future working in a casino for a slightly cocky, opinionated, won't take any crap kind of a guy with a dodgy attitude? Probably not.

I wanted something more, though. I had kept telling myself that I was better than this down the years just to keep me sane. All good things will come to those who wait but how long are you suppose to wait? What struck me the most as I stood there watching the deadbeats placing their bets was why had I spent almost nine years in this industry. It all seemed such a sad, colossal waste of time. So much potential and so little to show for it.

But that has always been my story ever since my final couple of years at school. The brightest kid in my year and now an IQ approaching Mensa level and what has it got me? Somebody once said that intelligence without application was merely unfulfilled potential and how right they were.

There are so many things that annoy me about working inside a small time casino. The quality of the punters is really only the beginning. I could spend all night talking about crap pay, no tips, working nights and unprofessional managers who think that they work at Caesar's Palace. The general manager walks past and gives me that same old look that says: "Stop talking to the dealer and do your job properly!" That guy really annoys me with his stuck up attitude; he thinks he's Donald Trump. With about fifty quid on each table, the dealer and me could handle this blindfolded.

I hear a huge cheer behind me and turn around to see the dealer isolating number 17 with a mountain of chips on it. The table had done about two grand in as far as I could tell in the past ten minutes. No big deal but evidently big enough for a floor manager to come and stand at the end of the table. Why do they do that? Why can't they see how bad that looks to punters? But why change the habits of a lifetime? They just continue to do what they have always done.

I look back to see Mr Boring English Guy place £2 on first and second dozens for what must be the 500th time tonight. He's even wearing a wedding ring; some woman must be wondering what she's done wrong having him for a husband. The dealer catapults the ball around the wheel at warp speed; there is no need for the ball to be travelling at that pace, but do I care? I didn't care nine years ago and I doubly don't care on what should be my final ever spin supervising roulette.

I keep saying to myself that if I ever let myself come back into gaming then I am just as deserving of a bullet to the head as some of the utter low life that frequent these places. The dealer announces "three, red, odd" and begins to isolate the number and clear the layout, but I am hardly watching. My head is elsewhere, filled with the thoughts of what adventures a change of career would bring. Truth was, I was not even sure if I was doing the right thing. I had secured a job as a trainee financial consultant with a respectable firm but I was only getting a basic salary for the first couple of months; after that it was commission only and I would be well and truly on my own.

The dealer cashed in the last of the bets and finally, after nine very long years, that was that. Just one final roulette table to cash in and I would be out of here. My poker buddy Darren who had been dealing the game asked what I would be doing.

"I'm going to work as a financial adviser Darren," I said, without wanting to elaborate any further or gloat about the fact that I was leaving and he wasn't. Darren was a good kid and a good footballer too, by all accounts, although I had never seen him play.

"Is that like pensions and insurance and stuff?"

"Yeah, really boring."

At that moment the pit boss came across to shake me by the hand and wish me all the best. We shook hands warmly. Scott was another one who I liked but he seemed destined to be a lifer. But the entire night had that feel of the final day in prison before release and I somehow felt a little guilty that I was leaving and the rest of them were not.

I looked around and suddenly it dawned on me what I was really going to miss about this job: the friendships and the camaraderie with fellow dealers and supervisors – this was the only thing that had kept me in this career for so long. With the tables cashed in and the pit in relative silence compared with the mayhem of a few minutes ago, we had the nightly ritual of waiting around on reception for the cabs to turn up. It seemed to take forever but turn up they did.

Suddenly the doors were opened and into the cool morning air we all strode like tired fed up troopers all bar one…me. My life was no longer dull and repetitive. No more was I perfectly aware of what tomorrow had in store for me. For the first time in ages, there was uncertainty, excitement and a dash of danger thrown in to my life, and I actually liked it.

August 2nd 1998

"Excuse me, is this seat taken?" I looked up to see some bearded geezer who was a dead ringer for Henry VIII staring down at me. I felt like saying yes because I was not overly keen on having a 20 stone sweating lump invading my personal space for what might turn out to be the next two hours. Before I had a chance to think, I blurted out "No, be my guest!" Would I live to regret it I wonder?

This train journey to Bournemouth for my three-week financial training course was scheduled to take about five hours and I had to change trains in Birmingham. I hoped there would be no delays on this trip as I hate travelling at the best of times. My girlfriend had come to see me off and she stood on the platform waiting for the train to depart. I'd only been seeing her for a few weeks but it seemed like forever. To be honest, I was glad to be away from her because she was irritating me greatly.

She was on the rebound and still hung up on some loser called Reggie – we had been a disaster as a couple from the start. We were only about ten minutes into the journey and already I'm restless. King Henry had dozed off almost straight away – how do people manage to go to sleep that fast? After about an hour, the long walk to the refreshment coach seemed like an adventure day out.

I never could sleep on journeys, but then I've always been a lousy sleeper anyway. As I returned to my seat with a can of coke, I remembered all the reading material that I had packed into my sports holdall. I had brought ten books with me and everyone of them on blackjack. I can't make my mind up if that is sad or being focused.

Focused on what though? I had the knowledge to hit the casinos hard; it was highly unlikely that anybody in the country knew what I did about blackjack. But let's be realistic, jack shit was going to happen because I didn't have the money to back myself and naturally cautious guys like me don't play professional blackjack anyway, they don't have the guts for it. However, that didn't stop me from reading about other guys doing it, and I settled down to read *Million Dollar Blackjack* by the late Ken Uston, once again.

Time seems to fly by whenever I am reading and studying blackjack although often that time is me day dreaming of what might be. King Henry appeared to be stirring from his slumber as the train ground to a jarring halt at some small town station that I had never heard of. I was not even aware that the train was supposed to stop here.

I put the book down, and looked out of the window briefly. As I did so, I saw King Henry scrutinising the front cover of my book. He realised that I had noticed him and felt that this gave him the opportunity to bombard me with questions about it.

"Interesting book?"

"Yeah!" I replied curtly.

Not to be put off by my obvious desire to not communicate, King Henry asked me if I played much.

"Not really but I did deal the game for nine years." Fatal error: I had now provided our Henry with precisely the kind of opportunity he had been looking for.

"What, you mean in a real casino?" was his next and obvious question.

What had I done? If this guy was going all the way to Bournemouth then I was doomed because he looked to me as if he was desperate for a mate. He slowly leaned across, obviously preparing to whisper something in my ear. He got so close that I could smell his cheap aftershave mingling with the odour of his sweating armpits.

"I have a system for blackjack! Care to hear it?"

Oh god not another blackjack expert, I'd seen and heard thousands down the years and now I'm stuck next to one, and we are not even at Birmingham yet. Then I remembered, I had to change trains in Birmingham and that was in about 15 minutes' time. Suddenly the world seemed a brighter place and I casually replied, "Go on then, what is it?"

The first meeting, August 7th 1998

Less than five days into this course I was already having severe reservations about the move that I was making. I didn't like the people and at no point felt comfortable in their company. I was being paid reasonably well for this three-week induction and was seriously considering jacking it in at the end and just taking the money. Never comfortable wearing ties and suits, I kept telling myself that if I was ever going to make anything of my life then I was just going to have to get my head down, and stop all this silent whinging. But it was difficult. There were two guys on the course who were incredibly annoying. I kept picturing what their heads would look like after being mauled by a bull terrier.

On the Friday we took the lunch break earlier than usual. I had a train scheduled at 3pm to take me home for the weekend. Not that I had anything particular to go home to, but these people were pissing me off and I needed some breathing space.

Walking down the corridor in the direction of the canteen, the incredibly annoying Peter sidled up to me and asked what plans I had for the weekend.

"I need to pop back home, Peter, to take care of a bit of business." I was lying through my teeth but it was all I could think of at the time.

"Not staying with us then for a bit of company bonding?" was his reply.

I smiled and merely answered "Afraid not." What I actually felt like saying was "Get real, I'd rather eat camel shit."

I hated lunchtimes because I felt obliged to sit and eat food at the same table as these halfwits and pretend to be friendly. To be fair, it was not that they were bad people, they were just totally different from me and I must confess to missing my mates from the casino – most of whom didn't have chips on their shoulders and inflated egos like many of these people on the course.

I turned away from the checkout with my food tray to find that the suit and tie brigade table was full, as Peter had taken the final seat. At least I could eat in peace now, without any more remarks about my northern accent or having to listen to how superior London is compared with the rest of the country.

I was just starting to tuck into my lasagne and chips when someone asked if he could sit down.

"Be my guest," I replied, as I looked up to see a rather well-rounded guy in his mid to late 40s. We made small talk for about five minutes. He told me that he was in Bournemouth on business, without actually volunteering what it was, and I never asked.

"Mike tells me that you used to work in casinos as a croupier." Mike Hanlon was the guy who was in charge of our course and it was apparent that these two knew each other well.

"Yeah that's right, for nine long years…something of a misspent youth."

My companion introduced himself as Steve and remarked how he was a very keen punter, which was surprising, as most people do not like to admit that they frequent such places. To my surprise, Steve was very well travelled (in a gaming sense) and had been in many casinos up and down the country. Travelling and staying in hotels was a large part of this man's life and he obviously wasn't one for staying in his room all night, either. "Come on then. Do the casinos cheat? Is it rigged?"

I had lost count of the number of times that I had been asked this. I think the curiosity stems from the fact that many people's only experience of such places is from watching TV.

"No, they have no reason to because the odds built into the games defeat the player in the long run, without them having to do anything crooked." There is absolutely no point in going into all of the ways that a player can win inside a casino in a five-minute conversation; most of them involve cheating anyway.

"What's the best game to play then?" he asked.

"Blackjack, without any shadow of a doubt," was my instant reply. Of course if you happen to be cheating or colluding or both, then all games can be good. By this time we had both finished our food, but that didn't prevent him from persevering with the questions.

"So if you went into a casino, could you win?" inquired Steve.

"That's not a straightforward question to answer," I said, trying to be as thorough as possible.

I asked him if he meant beating the casino on the level or cheating, to which he replied "Both!"

"Yes, I could earn a lot of money hitting casinos."

He looked at me in a way that suggested that he didn't entirely believe me. He smirked, and said "Why aren't you doing it then?"

For once, I gave him a straightforward answer and didn't beat about the bush: "Because I don't have the funding," I replied. "Winning big inside a casino is not like the national lottery, you can't turn a quid into millions overnight!"

We finished our lunch and he asked me how long I was down there for.

"I have two more weeks after this one, but I'm catching a train home for the weekend at three o'clock."

He inquired how far I had travelled and it turned out that we only lived about 25 miles apart. He got up to leave, saying "Probably see you next week."

"Yeah, see you," I replied.

The meeting with Steve had gone right out of my head by the time I boarded the train. I was glad to be away from it all and the thought of returning to normality seemed like paradise. I must have been very tired because, for once, I actually slept.

August 21st 1998

At last I had reached the end of this damn course; it had felt like an ordeal to me from day one. All the group members exchanged pleasantries with each other and vowed to keep in touch...yeah right! All our things were already packed and in the store room so there was no need to go back to the hotel. As I was leaving the lecture room, I walked up to Mike and thanked him for all his help. We shook hands. Mike was a good bloke and he had been one of the few bright spots for me on this trip.

"I have something for you, Carl." I was puzzled as I had not seen Mike give anything to anybody else. He handed me a small white business card and I was surprised to see that it was Steve's. "He would like you to give him a call when you get back." I thanked Mike and shook his hand again. On the train home, I immersed myself in the works of Stanford Wong, who is one of the leading theoreticians in blackjack. Once again, I would dream of the double agent lifestyle of a professional blackjack player...I wondered what Steve wanted with me.

CHAPTER 2

WHERE'S THAT BUSINESS CARD?

October 1998

From this point on, the dates begin to get a little hazy so I will only refer to months. Pensions and life insurance was beginning to bore me silly. I was finding it hard to put the time in because my heart simply wasn't in it. The guys that I was mixing with here just seemed the same as those who had been on my three-week induction…stuck up bores!

I was a working-class kid who had come from a rough council estate; I'd had solid, down to earth, working-class parents. I hated feeling uncomfortable with these people and all I ever seemed to do was chase the clock around all day wishing that I was somewhere else. Battling through rush hour traffic was another first for me: where in god's name have all these cars come from? For nine years, I never ever witnessed that volume of traffic as I had usually been in bed after a night shift during the rush hour.

Some asshole cut me up without even indicating. I blew my horn in frustration and he just gave me the rods. I would have killed the bastard if I could have got my hands on him. I finally arrived home at 6pm and went straight to the fridge because I was starving, just like I always was after work. I switched on the evening news to catch the end of a story, which is something to do with casinos. Suddenly, like a flash of light, I remembered Steve's business card and how he had asked Mike to ask me to give him a call when I got back off the course.

But that was two months ago. An awful lot of water had gone under the bridge since then and it felt awkward to call after all this time. I looked through the TV guide to see if there was anything of interest for me to watch but, as usual, utter crap! If there had been anything decent to watch then I probably wouldn't have made the call. After taking quite some time to find Steve's card, I must confess I felt slightly nervous about picking up the phone.

I almost hung up because it took Steve what seemed like forever to answer and I thought that no one was at home.

"Hello Steve speaking", a couple of seconds must have passed as I was working out what to say.

"Hi Steve, it's Carl from Bournemouth."

There was another slight pause as he was obviously struggling to remember who I was. *"Carl!!* Long time no hear, I thought that you had lost my number."

We made small talk for about ten minutes with him basically asking me questions about how my change of career was going. I told him that I thought that I had made a big mistake in changing jobs and was seriously considering going back to casinos. Again, I got the impression from Steve's tone that there was some other purpose to him making conversation with me. I felt it down in Bournemouth and I was feeling it now. People like him didn't want to be friends and associate with people like me, it was that simple. "Do you remember, Carl, how we talked about blackjack?"

Here we go I thought, he's about to try to get me involved in something really dodgy. "Vaguely" was my guarded reply, knowing full well that I could remember the conversation almost word for word.

"I may have need of your expertise and I would like to pick your brains."

I sat and listened to Steve go into detail about how he was contemplating setting up a team of "top hatters" to hit the casinos at roulette. This is known as "past posting" in other parts of the world but "top hatting" is just a variation of it. It is simply a method of placing a bet on roulette after the ball has dropped into the number.

It is team play and other team members usually try to cause some kind of diversion to allow the bettor the opportunity to get the bet down. Let's not beat around the bush here, this is cheating plain and simple. Steve wanted me along purely in an advisory capacity because he felt that someone with the kind of gaming experience that I had would be able to make the tactic work better.

"I don't think it's a great idea Steve," I replied. I cannot recall the exact conversation but these are my reasons against doing something like this, and they applied to Steve and any other potential "Top Hatters" out there who think that they are doing something smart. First, casino staff – at least experienced ones – are so well versed in this tactic that it is almost obsolete. Even if the dealer is inexperienced, the supervisor (known as an inspector in England) simply by definition will have considerable experience.

Second, new faces always stand out a mile and cheats who attempt this kind of thing do not realise how obvious they are. Staff know who their regulars are and new faces stick out like a sore thumb, so they are half expecting a move anyway. Third, even if the move is successful, the payout could be delayed so that CCTV footage is inspected. Staff will do this merely on suspicion and that's before you can even get to cash desk and out of the door with the money.

Finally, having me there at all could be a disaster. After all, I am ex-gaming and casino staff tend to be very widely travelled with most of them having worked in other casinos during their careers. I was nine full years in that job, which essentially means that a lot of people know me, including literally thousands of punters. Information is passed from casino to casino and even passed between rival companies because they all share a common goal – to protect themselves against cheats.

Steve listened intently to everything that I had to say without interrupting once. When I had finished, he paused for a few seconds before saying "But you said that you could beat the casinos if you ever went back and that all you lacked was the money."

I remember thinking how good this guy's memory was and he had obviously paid very careful attention to everything that I had said at our first meeting: "Yes I did say that, Steve, and I also said, if you recall, that it would be on blackjack where I would do it."

"So how much could you take the casinos for if you had the money?"

This was the kind of question that was impossible to answer accurately. It depended on so many factors coming together, of which the most important are the quality of team members, bankroll size and the level of anonymity: "I think that serious damage could be done with a bankroll of fifty thousand but one hundred grand would be better." With a bankroll of 200 big bets, £100,000 would enable any team to bet as much as £500 on a hand. But the strategies that I would use would mean a greater edge than conventional counting and £100,000 would be more than adequate.

"If the strategies are so powerful then why do you need so much money?"

This is a question that any would be backer is bound to ask and the answer is rather simple although complex to the novice.

I explained about standard deviation and the variance that is built into the game and the anticipated results that can be expected when certain types of advantage are secured. Much of it seemed to sink in but I could tell from some of Steve's answers that I had also confused him in some areas. I basically told him that if he was thinking of setting up a team then blackjack was the game to attack and not by using a move that casino staff were well versed in, which would have a limited shelf life anyway.

Steve seemed to take on board what I had said and then he asked me if I would care to meet him and two of his colleagues, one of whom was a card counter by all accounts. "I would like it if they heard what you had to say, Carl, because they understand this stuff far better than me." I had no problem with meeting anybody because I knew full well that my expertise would stand the Pepsi-challenge with anyone, least of all some run of the mill counter.

There was one burning question that I had been wanting to ask him for some time and that was just what plans he had in mind.

"Well to be honest, Carl, you have impressed me tremendously with what you have said and it takes an awful lot to impress me." It was flattering for a successful businessman openly to admit that I impressed him, but what he said next knocked me for six: "I would like to finance you to play blackjack for me, Carl. Would you do it?"

This was it, the chance that I had been waiting for. It sounded like music to my ears, but I suddenly started crapping myself. "It's not as straightforward as that, Steve. A lot of stuff needs to be sorted out."

He looked at me in a puzzled kind of a way and asked: "Like what?"

"Well first, like I said before, I'm ex-gaming and that is always a danger. Second, even if I could pull it off, individual counters stand out far more than a team does."

Steve looked at me for a few seconds then asked, "If you were not ex-gaming could you do it?"

I replied that I certainly could. The techniques and tactics that we would be using not only would give us a return on turnover of about 4 or 5 per cent but also would be very difficult to spot.

"So what you are saying is that you can't do it because you are too well known?"

I told him that was basically it in a nutshell. "It's not that it would be impossible, Steve, just too risky, that's all. But the ideal way around that problem would be for me to train and then supervise the team."

"A couple of friends of mine really know their stuff about blackjack."

I didn't know quite what he meant by that and, not wanting to lose out on an opportunity, I quickly replied, "Card counting is not enough these days to beat blackjack all by itself because the games are poor and the penetration is bad in many casinos."

Steve asked what "penetration" meant to which I carefully informed him that it was the number of cards that were dealt out of a blackjack shoe before the cutting card was reached. Casinos tend to deal short shoes as a counter measure against knowledgeable players or sometimes merely because a table is losing, which is utter nonsense. Many dealers do it, though, because it gives them a breather in between shoes or if they fancy a chat with the inspector. "So you see Steve, you really need to hit them with weapons that are more powerful than counting."

"Such as?"

"Well, shuffle tracking for one. I have a computer program at home that tracks any casino shuffle and locates the positions of certain clumps of cards after the shuffle. The software is fantastic but it is very complex to use. I have it installed on my lap-top." I was lying through my teeth about the software being complex because I was afraid of showing these guys too much and have them then cut me out of the equation. Besides, there are not many teams who can take on the casinos even at black-jack and get away with it for long enough periods to really make it pay; they simply get caught. At the end of the day, technical knowledge counts for jack if you get caught and the greatest skill to blackjack is pulling it off. This gets harder to do the higher you play so from where I was sitting they needed me anyway.

I could detect the excitement in Steve's voice as I told him about the software and he sounded like the kid who had just been handed the keys to the sweet cupboard. "What's so good about shuffle tracking, Steve, is that you end up placing bets at times when conventional counters wouldn't, like at the begin-ning of a shoe for instance. No card counter is going to increase their bet or max out when they haven't got any count informa-tion yet."

"So what's the other stuff that you said was powerful?"

"I'm afraid that starts to get into a grey area because many of the moves are strictly cheating."

"So where's the grey area? Either it's cheating or it isn't, Carl."

I laughed out loud and said "It's cheating, but I think that we ought to stick to counting and tracking."

"But I thought that you said that card counting was not very effective these days."

"It isn't, but you still need a base to work from and you need to count to be able to shuffle track."

We agreed that we ought to meet to have a discussion about the practicality of setting up a team with Steve's two accom-plices, whoever they were, and then take it from there. Steve asked if I would bring my laptop with the shuffle tracking software to show his friends and I quickly agreed. Steve inquired if I was free the following Wednesday because that was the ideal day for John and Kevin, his two "advisers".

"Wednesday sounds fine to me, Steve, what time?"

We agreed on 7pm at his house and, after Steve gave me directions, ended the conversation. After I had put the phone down, I could feel my heart thumping from the excitement. I couldn't believe that some guy who I had hardly met was offering to back me to the tune of 100K. It was then that a serious dose of reality started to kick in. These guys may be trying to con me or something or perhaps they are going to use my knowledge and then blow me out.

Still, what had I got to lose? Even if they were just using me then all it was going to cost was a bit of my time and the cost of the petrol going to Steve's house. It all felt too good to be true on reflection, and I went to bed that evening having come down considerably from cloud nine, but then, I've always been a pessimist!

Here we go

What the hell is a matter with me? There was about 30 minutes before I was due to begin the short journey to Steve's house and I was starting to doubt myself. Do I really have the knowledge to beat the casinos when push comes to shove? Maybe Steve's two accomplices knew more than me, maybe they will make me look stupid. That ultra cautious alter ego of mine was starting to rear its ugly head once again.

I had made doubly sure that I was well versed with the software on the laptop because I had the excellent count analyser installed, which did all sorts of marvellous things, the best of which predicted earn rates for various counts and strategies and calculated the standard deviation as well.

I began to run through what I might need in my mind for this meeting. Don't forget the lead for the laptop in case the battery is a bit low, I told myself. I ran through in my head just what I was going to say but I had been doing that for several days, anyway. I had not gone into work for three days, much to the annoyance of my sales manager, who had told me that I needed to redouble my efforts if I was going to succeed. He was someone else who really annoyed me.

I realise that I might come across as someone who doesn't like anybody and that I am totally anti-social, but that is not the case at all. I just missed the friendship of the more down to earth guys in the casino. I set off for the meeting early, just like I always do for important events, because I get paranoid about being late.

The journey itself took about 45 minutes and I found Steve's house without any problem as his directions were excellent, and he didn't live far from the M1. The house was impressive. It looked like a mansion compared with what I lived in, and my Ford Escort looked like a pauper's car parked next to his Jaguar XK8, which had a personalised plate.

The path that led up to the front door must have been 50 yards long and I started thinking about why this guy was interested in blackjack and "Top Hatting" on roulette, when he had so much obvious wealth. But maybe he was broke; maybe all this rich living had taken its toll and he needed the money but didn't have the drive or desire to want to work hard for it. But surely people like him could earn money at the drop of a hat? I still didn't really know what he did for a living.

I knocked at the door and Steve answered almost immediately: "I saw you come up the drive; you're a bit early, Carl." As it turned out John and Kevin had not arrived yet but it was only 6.45pm so they were by no means late.

"Come on in."

Steve led me down a long corridor into the lounge and as I

looked around at the lavish furnishings and decor, I couldn't help thinking that this guy had some serious wealth. "Tea or coffee?" he asked.

I replied, "Coffee please, white with one sugar."

While Steve was in the kitchen fixing the drinks, the doorbell rang. As he answered, I could tell from the initial conversation that this was John and Kevin. It sounded as if they all knew each other well and this made me feel like something of an outsider.

They must have been talking in the kitchen for about five minutes. It was nothing secretive as I could hear the entire conversation, but it did start to heighten my nerves a bit more. I knew full well that I was going to be on trial here and if I was going to get anywhere with this then I was going to have to sell myself and my product seriously. But wait a minute, what the fuck do I know about sales technique? Then I remembered how Steve had wanted me to be a part of his "Top Hatting" team simply because I had worked inside a casino previously. This meant that they were attaching an awful lot of weight to the fact that I was ex-gaming and seemed very keen to beat the casinos at something, irrespective of what.

The three of them walked into the room and I stood to shake John and Kevin by the hand. Kevin was a tall guy in his early 50s, with short thinning hair and glasses. John seemed a bit older, with grey hair and a moustache. He was slightly porky. I could sense them sizing me up immediately and, of course, I was doing the same to them.

Most of the conversation that I had overheard when they were in the kitchen had been to do with horse racing and the stock market, so it seemed little surprise to me that these guys were into beating casinos in some way. I politely inquired which of them was a counter, and Kevin replied that he was, which confused me a bit because Steve said that both of them were.

I asked him what counting system he had been using and he

replied that he had used the Advanced Omega 2.

"That's a good count, did you find the ace side count easy" I asked.

"Yeah it was fairly straightforward" replied Kevin.

All counting systems are designed to identify situations where there is a preponderance of high cards and aces remaining in the shoe. This gives the edge to the player and that edge varies depending on what the count is and how many cards are left to be dealt. It was obvious from the initial conversation that Kevin was by far the more chatty and confident of the two. John seemed fairly reserved.

Changing the conversation slightly, I looked at Steve and asked him what he did for a living. Kevin and John smiled at each other and Steve replied that he was an "entrepreneur." He wasn't volunteering any more than that so I didn't push the matter. There was obviously a lot more to Steve than met the eye and he probably didn't feel comfortable in divulging certain things to me yet.

"You took an awful chance, Steve. in telling me your plans about the Top Hatting. I could have still been in contact with people on the inside for all you knew, and grassed you up."

"Possible but very doubtful. I had you sussed, Carl, from the first meeting." He smirked, suggesting that he had the self-confidence of a man who knew full well that I was unlikely to have divulged what we had talked about to anyone else.

"Right, shall we get down to business then?" said John.

Before we go any further with what was discussed in that meeting, I am going to give those that need it, a tutorial in card counting and playing blackjack that will take you above and beyond nearly all blackjack players on the planet. This is not because the information in the next chapter is revolutionary, it is just that so many players even today are totally ignorant of it, so get ready for a little lesson.

CHAPTER 3

BLACKJACK 101

The theory behind card counting has been around since the 1960s. In fact the earliest counters go back beyond even that. But we have Ed Thorp to thank for the explosion in blackjack when his classic book *Beat the Dealer* first hit the shelves. Much has happened in blackjack since those early days and many new and more powerful counting systems have been devised in addition to the ones that Thorp talks about in that book.

Card counting systems

The High-Low count

Card counting systems increase in complexity from the basic Level 1 counts to the far more complex Level 4 systems. A Level 1 system basically adds and subtracts in units of one depending on what cards are dealt and a Level 2 system adds or subtracts in units of one or two, and vice versa. The counting system that I will be showing you here will be the Level 1 "High-Low count".

This is the counting system that we used and it was very effective for our purpose. The great strength of the High-Low is in fact its simplicity. This counting system was shunned by many professionals as being too weak and not identifying enough advantageous situations. But as the game has moved into the 21st century, and it has become clear that counting knowledge will not do the job by itself, irrespective of the system that is used, the simplicity of the High-Low enables the player to be able to do several things at once, including shuffle track.

I used to practise this count and many others when I was a croupier but the complicated Level 3 and Level 4 counts made it difficult for me to concentrate on anything else but the counting. Being able to track the count and carry on a conversation with someone at the same time adds an awful lot of deception to your play. Another advantage to using a simpler count is that mental fatigue takes much longer to set in, so your playing sessions are not only longer but also much more error free.

The basics behind not just the High-Low but all card counting systems is to identify when the player has the edge and when the casino has the edge. They do this by awarding each card denomination a numerical value. I am assuming that you already know the rules of blackjack so I will not be expanding on that here. When the un-dealt portion of the deck is richer in high cards and aces than it is low cards, then the player has the edge, and vice-versa.

The numerical values that the High-Low gives to each card are as follows. Cards 2, 3, 4, 5 and 6 are given a total of +1 every time they are dealt. Cards 7, 8 and 9 are counted as 0 because they are neither good nor bad for the player, whenever they appear. All picture cards and aces are awarded a total of −1. If you are confused by this minus total for the high cards and aces, remember that if a dealer has dealt an ace, for example during a round of play, then that card cannot be dealt to your box in the future so the advantage of having it still remaining in the shoe has disappeared.

The running count
As the cards are dealt, you need to keep a continuous count,

which is known as the "running count". For example, let's say on the first round of play after the shuffle that you have seen the cards 4, 10, 6, 7, 10, 10, 10, A, 5, 8, 2 (picture cards count as 10). The running count for these 11 cards is −1. This is the cumulative total of adding and subtracting 1 based on the totals that I showed you previously.

This accumulative total (the "running count") is not enough by itself to ascertain whether the player has got the edge. This is because the rules of the game dictate that the house always starts with an edge at the beginning of a shoe. This edge is in the region of 0.5 per cent for the game of blackjack as it is played in England, with the rule variations that we have over here. So for instance if the first five cards that were dealt out of a new shoe were all low value cards (2 to 6), the running count would be +5.

Now this does not mean that the player has an edge…Yet! This is where many people who are learning to count go hugely wrong. The ratio of high cards to low cards must reach a certain level for an advantage to be secured. To explain this further, I will give a little example. Take for instance two situations where the running count is +5, one where the first five cards to be dealt out of the shoe have all been low and the other where the final five cards to be dealt are all high cards or aces.

The running count is +5 in both examples, but in the second one, you stand a 100 per cent chance of having a 10 or an ace as your next card if you happen to have the first box. This is one of the reasons why many casinos have a cutting card, so that this kind of advantage for the player is never reached. This ratio of high cards:low cards to cards left to be dealt needs to be measured. One very common method is to take the count, let's say it is +10, and then to divide it by the number of decks remaining.

For example, we have a four-deck game where exactly two decks have been dealt and two decks remain. This is easy enough to ascertain even if the shoe has a lid, because all you have to do is take a subtle look at the discards and the remaining decks can be figured out from that. So in this instance, we take our running count of +10 and divide it by the number of decks remaining to be dealt – two – to get a new total of +5.

The true count

This new figure is called the "true count" and is a far more accurate reflection of when the player has the edge and by how much. It is the true count and not the running count that is used to ascertain when to up the bet or bet at all, and when to reduce the bet or not to bet at all, whichever the case may be. Always remember that at the beginning of the shoe, the casino starts out with an edge of roughly 0.5 per cent for the game as it is played over here.

For every true count point increase or decrease, that edge fluctuates by roughly 0.5 per cent. This means that the true count has to reach +1 for the player to be breaking even with casino, and +2 for them to have a 0.5 per cent advantage. This also works when the count goes negative. If the true count is −1 the dealer has a 1 per cent edge and not the original 0.5 per cent that it was at the beginning of the shoe.

The balanced count

The high-low system is what is known as a balanced count. This means that if you have counted the deck correctly, the count will always return to 0 from when you first started. This is because the number of cards in the deck that have a positive value mirror exactly the number of cards that have a negative value.

Card counting in its entirety is a very complex subject and is almost like science and art combined: the science is the mathematics behind the thing, the art is the deception. There is no doubt that the art to card counting is not in actually doing it, which can be done by anyone with average intelligence who has gotten hold of a decent book. It is getting away with it that is the real skill, especially in situations where gaming staff are knowledgeable.

Game selection

Another vastly underrated skill in blackjack is game selection. Game selection is critical in games like poker as well; in fact many facets of blackjack and poker are remarkably similar. Game selection is of much greater importance for pure counters than it is for shuffle trackers and exponents of some of the other moves that you will read about in this book.

If you are to beat blackjack in England in the 21st century that is dealt from a shoe, then you really need everything to be perfect in order for card counting to be successful merely on its own. For instance, there is a high proportion of six-deck games in England. This means six decks of cards that are shuffled together. The earning potential of a counter in a six-deck game is significantly less on average than it is for a four-deck game.

There are complex reasons behind this, which I am not going into, because it is not the purpose of this book, but trust me when I say that it is true. The rule variations for blackjack differ the world over: they are not universal. Let me tell you that the rules for the game as it is played in England are not that good for the player.

There are numerous other factors as well that combine to make a game either more or less profitable. One of the most important is game speed. If you happen to be stuck on the only available table that is open in the casino (very common in England especially in the afternoon) and it is being dealt by a slow, cumbersome, trainee dealer then this will seriously impede your earning rate. So too will a jam-packed table. I have witnessed some games where no more than 30 hands per hour were being dealt.

Penetration

Another important factor that seems to evade new counters is the importance of penetration. I have already explained what this means but the importance of it cannot be underestimated. If you happen to be counting a game and the dealer is constantly cutting the deck in half and only dealing two decks out of four or three decks out of six then you are basically wasting your time. You could try subtly pointing out that you have come to play blackjack and not to watch the dealer shuffle.

Be careful though if you say this, because you do not want to upset the dealer nor want them to think that you have some kind of vested interest in dealing out more cards from the shoe. As I said before, the main purpose of this book is not to teach readers how to count, but I felt that much of the value of reading it would be lost if counting and tracking knowledge were absent. There are some very good books on blackjack theory, which are excellent purchases if you wish to pursue this further. But pleased be advised one more time: blackjack counting knowledge all by itself will simply not get the job done. This will apply in many parts of the world and in fact many casinos in the UK now have shuffling machines, which totally eliminate the advantage that can be gleaned entirely from counting or shuffle tracking.

As a corollary to card counting, you must also know just what to do with each individual hand that you are dealt. You must know when to stand, hit, split and so on, because your own personal gut feelings or intuition about what cards are coming next have absolutely nothing whatsoever to do with it. This way of playing each individual hand is called "basic strategy".

Basic strategy

What follows is a generic basic strategy that is correct for the game as it is played in England and indeed many other locations as well. Basic strategy goes far beyond merely memorising the content of the following table and is in fact a very complex subject in its own right. There has been a phenomenal amount of work done on improving basic strategy over the years and many of the strategy decisions alter depending on what the count is.

This is because the decision on which way to play the hand is very close and it is the count itself that sometimes makes the decision for you. For instance, whether to hit or stand on 16 against a 10 depends on just what the count is. This is not the most accurate basic strategy but, again, going into the complexities of something that is a subject all by itself is not the point of this book.

Fortunately for us, Donald Schlesinger took most of the work out of memorising strategy deviations by inventing the "Illustrious 18". This was a list of the 18 most important deviations and just how important each one was. But giving you added basic strategy deviations to remember is pointless and much less important when you are shuffle tracking. The power of shuffle tracking when coupled with some of the other techniques that you will learn about in this book basically makes conventional counting almost obsolete anyway. But for the sake of completeness, here is "basic strategy". American readers will notice differences between the basic strategy in this chart and what they have been used to, especially the doubling of 11 and the splitting of aces. This is because of the rule that we have in the UK of losing all doubles and splits to a natural (a blackjack).

Pairs

Dealer's upcard

Your hand	2	3	4	5	6	7	8	9	10	A
A-A	SP	SP	SP	SP	SP	SP	SP	SP	SP	N
10-10	N	N	N	N	N	N	N	N	N	N
9-9	SP	SP	SP	SP	SP	N	SP	SP	N	N
8-8	SP	SP	SP	SP	SP	SP	SP	SP	N	N
7-7	SP	SP	SP	SP	SP	SP	N	N	N	N
6-6	SP	SP	SP	SP	SP	N	N	N	N	N
5-5	N	N	N	N	N	N	N	N	N	N
4-4	N	N	N	N	N	N	N	N	N	N
3-3	SP	SP	SP	SP	SP	SP	N	N	N	N
2-2	SP	SP	SP	SP	SP	SP	N	N	N	N

Key: SP = split; N = no (do not split)

Soft totals

Dealer's upcard

Your hand	2	3	4	5	6	7	8	9	10	A
A-9	S	S	S	S	S	S	S	S	S	S
A-8	S	S	S	S	S	S	S	S	S	S
A-7	S	S	S	S	S	S	S	H	H	H
A-6	H	H	H	H	H	H	H	H	H	H
A-5	H	H	H	H	H	H	H	H	H	H
A-4	H	H	H	H	H	H	H	H	H	H
A-3	H	H	H	H	H	H	H	H	H	H
A-2	H	H	H	H	H	H	H	H	H	H

Key: H = hit; S = stand

Hard totals

Dealer's upcard

Your hand	2	3	4	5	6	7	8	9	10	A
17	S	S	S	S	S	S	S	S	S	S
16	S	S	S	S	S	H	H	H	H	H
15	S	S	S	S	S	H	H	H	H	H
14	S	S	S	S	S	H	H	H	H	H
13	S	S	S	S	S	H	H	H	H	H
12	H	H	S	S	S	H	H	H	H	H
11	D	D	D	D	D	D	D	D	H	H
10	D	D	D	D	D	D	D	D	H	H
9	H	D	D	D	D	H	H	H	H	H
8	H	H	H	H	H	H	H	H	H	H

Key: H = hit; S = stand; D = double

So there you have it, the brief diversion to show the basics of card counting and playing each individual hand. I'm sure that many experienced counters will not have enjoyed reading something that they were already aware of but this book is not just meant for you now, is it?

Chapter 4

Getting Down to Business

October 1998, continued

"Right, shall we get down to business then?" asked John.

Everyone in the room looked at me and I knew that from this point onwards I was on stage. I asked Kevin how successful he had been at counting and he told me that he had done very well. Something about the way he said it told me that he was lying. There were still decent games out there back in 1998, but they had to be approached right, and this required substantial skill. I doubted that he had it.

"John is also a counter," said Steve.

I replied, "Oh right, that's very useful because it means I won't have to bother training anyone up." I smiled and everyone smiled back and laughed along, which kind of did wonders for my nerves, although I got the impression that John didn't like the idea of someone whom he barely knew knowing that he was a counter. After all, he had not spoken up earlier when I had asked which of them was a counter. I continued, "It's difficult to do any real damage with counting and especially over here where the rules and the penetration are rubbish."

John and Kevin both nodded. From my initial impressions of them they had a fair degree of counting knowledge between them, but they both lacked finesse from what I could see. John was only counting at a very low level inside his local casino and Kevin had been barred from counting at one club.

The fact that Kevin had been barred complicated matters a little bit and was something that I could have done without to be honest at this early stage. "I think that conventional blackjack will return 1 per cent on turnover at best and the variance is a killer," I said. It is possible for blackjack players to go very long periods while losing and this creates all kinds of mental pressures that become the downfall of many a good team.

John remarked, "I basically recycled money for years until the over-under came along." The over-under was a feature that appeared briefly on blackjack tables in the UK in the middle 1990s. It was a separate wager that could be placed by the player that the first two cards that they were dealt will either be lower or higher than 13. The casino took all tied bets. On the surface it was a dreadful bet for the punter if they were playing it on the level. But the feature could be blown out of the water not by traditional counting systems but by new powerful systems like the one devised by Arnold Snyder, which he famously dubbed the "Crush Count". Teams and individual counters from all over the UK and abroad hit the games and hit them hard during that golden period. The over-under feature was eventually removed but not after serious damage had been done by the pros.

"What if I told you that I could get you a 4 or 5 per cent return on turnover by going back to blackjack?"

Steve didn't look impressed by this statement as 5 per cent obviously didn't sound too much to him but John and Kevin knew full well what this meant, thank god. "5 per cent!" said John raising his voice.

"Is that good?" queried Steve.

"It's fucking sensational if it's true," said Kevin in his own subtle way.

"Remember that we are not talking about old-fashioned count-ing, shuffle tracking can get you three times the edge," I said.

"If it's only three times then surely that's only 3 per cent, is it not?"

Steve had obviously observed that I had earlier remarked that a 1 per cent turnover at best could be extracted from blackjack by traditional counting. This guy's memory was awesome when it came to remembering data. I replied "Some of the other tech-niques that I have will increase that substantially, for instance if you know that the next card is going to be a 10 on your box then that is a 13 per cent edge."

John and Kevin glanced at each other and as they did that I hit them with another statistic: "And it's over 50 per cent when that card is an ace."

"How do you know this?" asked John.

I simply winked at him, said, "It's called research old boy but first things first," and put the laptop onto the table in front of me.

"Carl has something very interesting that he wants to show you," remarked Steve. We arranged a table and chairs so that everyone could get a good view of the screen. It was all a bit cramped but nobody seemed to mind. The tension seemed to be heightened as everyone went quiet as the laptop fired up. At this point I would like to explain the concept of the software that I had on the computer.

Its entire purpose was for tracking shuffles and it was a great piece of software that literally tracked the path of the cards into the next shoe after they had been shuffled. Of course, there are many trackers out there that do this by visual estimation with no electronic help whatsoever. The problem with this is that it gets to be quite difficult when different dealers come to the table each with their own individual style and nuances.

To be honest when you reach a high level of skill in tracking, you are much better off doing it manually anyway, because you really need to keep a close eye on what the dealers are doing. This can only be done with the naked eye and can only be achieved by someone who is present.

In an ideal world, each casino or company should have their own individual house shuffle...in theory. But new staff tend to bring with them their own individual styles and habits, which can complicate the process immensely. If the tracking software is to work then the correct information must be put into it and even if the house shuffle is universal, each individual dealer differs when it comes to picking up certain amounts of cards during the shuffle. Some dealers shuffle half a deck while others only shuffle a quarter of a deck at a time. It is crucial to the process that this is observed and observed very well.

There are certain casinos that have far more complicated shuffles than others and some of the complications are designed to deter trackers by dispersing the cards more effectively. But no deck of cards can be randomly shuffled and certainly not by human hand in any reasonable time frame. The truth is that the casinos really cannot afford to spend too much time shuffling, because it costs them vast amounts of money when you multiply the effect of shuffling over time.

I remarked how most casinos had very basic shuffles, which could be tracked very easily. The hard part was detecting if any dealer was doing anything different on this particular shuffle from previous shuffles, because if they were and it was not detected by the tracker then that would be fatal. "The good thing about tracking is that you are going to be placing bets when any ordinary counter wouldn't, like at the start of the shoe." I was starting to get into my sales pitch but I was still over complicating the process of entering the shuffle into the computer, and this was deliberate.

The nagging feeling remained that after I had shown these guys what this software did, they might possibly go out and purchase it for themselves and then cut me out of the equation. These were my ideas and this was my dream, and I was not going to let a couple of know-it-all counters take it away from me. If only Kevin realised that getting barred was not clever or smart but just down right dumb. For any counter or tracker to get barred is not bad luck: it is bad preparation plain and simple.

Their eyes light up when the cards dispersed on the screen to highlight just where they would be in the next shoe. "Yeah but we can't take a laptop into a casino with us. I think they might just spot that," remarked Kevin in his usual sarcastic tone.

"No, but you can report the shuffle to me by mobile phone, then we can build a dossier on the dealers. You see, you can't play too long in anyone club anyway. This means travelling around and travelling around means that strangers are going to be entering casinos and strangers get looked at, especially strangers who are betting big on blackjack."

"Any ideas, Carl?" asked Steve.

"Yes I have. You see if strangers are going to be inside a casino then they need a valid reason to be there, because no punter is going to travel a hundred miles or so to play in a casino when they could go in any number of nearer ones and get the same action. Plus, people from the same area inside a casino one hundred miles away will set alarm bells ringing."

"So what's your idea then?" said John.

"Well it's basically twofold. You see, without meaning any offence, it is a totally different ball game when you start to play for big money." I was looking at John and Kevin when I said this. "From what you have told me neither of you has yet to play at a level that is going to attract serious attention and this is what I mean by a different ball game." I could tell that this last remark didn't go down too well with either of them but did I care? Did I hell because I was not here to make friends.

I continued, "This is why I think that going to a casino on the night of a poker tournament or some other big promotion will add an awful lot of cover, especially the poker tournaments. Back when I was in gaming, new punters always stood out unless it was poker night, when anyone who was unknown to the staff was presumed to have turned up just for the poker. You see, whenever there's a poker tournament, there will be cash games afterwards and sometimes the cash games can be quite big and this tends to attract people with money, even if the tournament itself isn't that big."

"So what's the other thing then?" asked Steve, looking on very intently.

"Well, one of the major things that traps counters and trackers, even very successful ones, is the fact that despite them covering their tracks as skilful players, winnings tend not to lie and the casino will cotton on very quickly to consistent winners, and will even share information with other clubs on this. This is why we need to move around an awful lot because once a pattern becomes evident then we are fucked, basically. I also want to use a strategy called the big player, but with modifications," I said.

"What's that?" remarked Steve.

John answered before I had a chance to speak: "It's where players count on the table and then signal in a non-playing partner."

"Why can't we just up our bets sitting there? That's what they have done for years," remarked Kevin.

"Because they are too aware of that, Kevin. They are not going to stand for anyone playing minimums and then eventually playing maximums irrespective of how innocent you make it look." The only way that this can be done is by increasing the bet after a run of winning hands, making it appear that you are gambling with winnings, but there is a risk if that run never comes or if it does not come at the right time.

"What you have got to remember is that no one in the gaming

industry or very few of them really understand advantage play at blackjack, and they will simply bar you on suspicion or fear without fully understanding what is actually going on. This is why I believe in the theory of doing everything out in the open. Edgar Allen Poe once said that the best place to hide anything was out in the open and this principle applies to what we are doing as well. I want the big player to be brash and loud and I especially want them to interact with the dealers and management. What we do not want is someone who is trying to go unnoticed."

I went on, "All three of you frequent casinos and are members all over the place so you will not be suspected, but if any one of you starts to do something that is out of character then that will get noticed very quickly, and by that I mean start to bet big." I was in full flow now and I had their full attention. Even the mouthy Kevin wasn't interrupting. "You see I have this idea of floating big players because repeatedly using the same big player on the same table as one or two players will also leave a pattern."

"What do you mean floating?" Asked Steve.

"Well, every casino has their own individual big players on roulette and blackjack. Some of these people will have been known to them for years and may even be friends with the management. Imagine for a minute how effective it would be to use a team of real big players who were already known to the casino. Each big player wouldn't be aware of the identity of the others and wouldn't even be aware of the size of the team they were playing in. Every time they went on a winning run, the casino would tolerate it because the players are well known to them and they would have gone on similar runs in the past anyway. Even if they suspected something, would they really want to risk upsetting a major punter on a suspicion before they could prove anything? By that time we would be gone and using another known big player in another area."

"That's fucking brilliant," remarked Kevin.

"But just how do we go about finding and approaching these people?" asked John.

"I know a couple of people who will be up for it," I said, to which Steve added that he new several people and he could approach numerous others, many of whom were down south.

I quickly stressed that these players had to be big hitters and not just someone who bet a hundred quid on a box from time to time. It had to be this way because if we were to earn any kind of real money out of this then we had to get a serious amount of money across the table in action, and it had to look natural to the bosses and the best way to do that is with known big punters.

Steve told me not to worry as he would check that out, but he knew full well that several of them fitted this description.

"Right, how good are you at bullshitting?" I directed this question at everyone and no one in particular. No one answered so I went on, "Because you are going to have to be someone else when you are playing the big players."

"This will not be a problem with the known big players, but if you want to be a big player, Steve, then you are going to have to play the part and that means getting into character."

"Take Patty with you," said Kevin, "Having a women on your arm is good cover."

This is of course very true as women and card counting do not seem to be associated with each other. This is blatantly wrong as many women have been successful counters and trackers, and have consistently slipped under the radar. But the fact remains that casinos just do not view women as much of a threat compared with the men. Patty was Steve's partner and had been for about four years, but they weren't married and didn't plan to get hitched as far as I knew.

We carried on the conversation. I demonstrated the software and all three of them marvelled at its complexity and power despite the fact that it only ran on MS DOS which is antiquated by today's standards. In fact many young kids won't even know what MS DOS is, although not being a computer geek, I would struggle to explain it anyway.

"You mentioned earlier about huge edges when you know what the next card is," said John.

"That's right," I said.

"So just how do you get to know what the next card is?" asked John.

"We can do this by using certain techniques, but by far the easiest is when dealers expose cards. You have all been inside casinos and you have all witnessed dealers making errors," I said. I looked at them and all three nodded in recognition. "Well, the casinos get away with an awful lot when many of these mistakes go unpunished. I have seen even experienced gaming staff clear wrong numbers on roulette that have cost the casino thousands. Many of these mistakes are because of over confident dealers who think that they have the ability to deal the game faster than they actually can."

I went on, "They only begin to realise their own inadequacies once they have fucked up. I remember one incident on blackjack when we had the over-under back in the 1990s. This particular dealer used to deal the cards really quickly, thinking that this somehow made her look good. One day, she had started with a soft total and got confused about her hand total halfway through. She had already got 17 and pulled another card. That card happened to be an ace."

To cut this story short, the rules in England state that any card that is accidentally pulled to the dealer's hand goes under the shoe and becomes the first card out on the next round of play. So not only did the player on first base know that their first card would be an ace, the rules of over-under stated that if you bet on the under and you were lucky enough to be dealt two aces then this paid 7-1. One very quick thinking punter bet to the maximum on first base because the ace gave him a guaranteed win on the under.

Low and behold, he was dealt another ace and the casino was taken to the cleaners with large amounts of egg on its face for good measure. I was not on this table as dealer or inspector but I observed it from the other side of the pit and I couldn't believe what I was witnessing. Just how a punter could have been allowed to get away with this amazes me even to this day.

All three of them shook their heads in astonishment. "So that actually happened!" said Kevin in a rather higher pitched voice than usual.

"Yeah and not only that, the same punter did it several more times," I said. "That's not all, this club also had a rule at that time that allowed players to cut any number of cards that they wanted on blackjack. The same geezer who did them on the over-under used to cut one card and one card only on blackjack, but get this. They didn't always have a cutting card at the back so a player only had to slightly move their head to see what the back card was and then if it was a 10 or an ace, simply cut it to the front so that it was the first card out of the shoe."

John and Kevin looked at each other in utter amazement: "Why weren't we playing in this club John?" asked Kevin.

John simply smiled and said, "Don't know but we should have been."

"They deserve to get fucked," said Steve, with which everyone agreed. All dealers make errors, some more than others. But if the average punter was aware of just what some of these errors meant in terms of mathematical edge then they wouldn't be as slow to capitalise on them. Some of the worst errors in blackjack and roulette occur because experienced dealers get complacent. Some of them spend so much time chatting to the punters or inspectors that they don't concentrate on the game properly.

"Many dealers get into bad dealing habits over the years and one of those habits is to apply too much pressure to the cards on blackjack when pulling them from the shoe, and this seems to apply more to male croupiers than female ones. Many dealers apply pressure to the centre of the card, which can actually make the next card out of the shoe visible to the player at first base, if they are low enough in their chair."

"Obviously not low enough to make it obvious," said Steve

"Obviously," said John

"When you couple this error with dealing too fast then certain dealers can become a fucking goldmine. Their eagerness to look good and deal fast can be used against them," I pointed out.

"Sounds to me that that would be an ideal job for Patty, because she's small anyway," said Kevin.

Steve grinned cheekily and pointed out that she would be up for anything especially if it got her away from the housework.

"Yeah but, is it not going to look odd if the big player waltzes in to play the maximum or close to it on someone else's box, surely they would want to play their own hand?" suggested John.

John was by far the more cautious of the two as far as I could see. I felt that if this was to go anywhere then Kevin may prove to be a bit of a loose cannon and potential trouble. He seemed the type not to like being told what to do, but then again I know someone else just like him!

"Not really, John," I said. "Once again it comes down to acting and bullshitting it's perfectly normal for a player to walk up to a table and not want to ruin any good run that the table is having by opening another box. Many players are very superstitious about that."

"Yes, but aren't they going to realise that something is wrong when every time the big player comes to the table, it's always the first box and the card is always a picture or an ace?" asked Steve.

"But it won't always be a picture or an ace, will it," I quickly responded. "Don't forget that this is just one strategy out of a battery of strategies. It's another string to our bow and will increase our profits, but it will not be the only tactic that we will be using. Remember we will not be card counting in the original sense, just counting so that we can locate where the high cards and aces will be during the next shoe. What would look odd though is if Patty was playing first base and Steve was the big player. They would possibly assume that Patty was counting for Steve and take steps based on that suspicion. Husband and wife teams have been done before so they would be on the lookout for that."

Kevin intervened, "Patty could go in as my partner. She's never been inside a casino. You two don't have the same name and you don't live together." If this actually came to pass, it would be ironic if Patty, who had never even been inside a casino before, let alone played in one, was responsible for winning more money for the team than John or Kevin, who had counted for years and had great experience between them playing blackjack.

Most casinos could be taken to the cleaners because of incompetent dealers and inspectors. The truth is that most staff are not even aware of their own incompetence. Most think that just because they have been in gaming since the year dot that they are the dog's bollocks when it comes to dealing. Most of them get sloppy because they are underpaid and pissed off in general. Many are bored through repetitive small action or just tired from working a double shift.

Most dealers don't watch the layout nearly as often as they should on roulette. They lower their guard because nothing ever happens night after night, and some think that the CCTV will deter any cheat anyway. In the casino where I worked, we had CCTV and I could still have taken the dealers for thousands had I been that way inclined, either as a member of staff or as a customer. The problem with all CCTV is that it is recording something that is three dimensional, but the picture is two dimensional so a lot of information is lost en route.

I knew where all the blind spots were and I knew exactly where I would have hit us had I been on the outside – and it was not always in the most obvious places either. The security inside the average casino in England is quite poor and every club is vulnerable. The staff can be the biggest threat if they have any level of intelligence at all. What makes it worse is that staff frequently get approached by unscrupulous punters to collude and cheat with them.

Most casinos have staff that indulge in after-hours drinking and the bars and clubs where they hang out become known to the rogues. What many of them fail to realise is that these cheats have been grooming them for ages, feeling them out psychologically. What they do not want to do is to approach a dealer to go into colluding with them only for that dealer then to grass them up. So they watch and listen, overhear conversations between staff and read body language. They can rapidly tell the career minded from the genuinely fed up and pissed off. There are not many happy staff inside casinos or at least there haven't been inside the ones where I have worked. The staff who laugh and joke with the managers only do it because they are two-faced.

I was once approached inside a 24-hour snooker club by a shady Iranian punter who tried to get me involved in some insurance scam that entailed me losing my job on purpose. I was also approached to collude and cheat. I should have reported these incidents, but most staff never do what they are supposed to do anyway.

I must have gone out with half a dozen female punters during my final couple of years in the job. This is strictly taboo but I didn't care by that time. I was so fed up with the job that the general manager could have caught us in bed for all I cared. This happens in every casino; staff socialise with punters outside work quite often, but the management never find out.

So the bottom line is that the management only knows a fraction of what is actually going on under their own roof. They are massively vulnerable and they know it, especially on roulette. We all know that there is no system that has ever been invented that can beat roulette. But who's talking about systems, for heaven's sake? Roulette has so many potential weaknesses that it is no surprise that the management gets so paranoid about it.

"There's another way to get to know what the first card is as well," I said.

They all looked on without anyone saying a word. I reached into my pocket and took out the three decks of cards that had been in there. I opened them, took out the jokers then shuffled them and cut them into two equal halves. "Right, let's pretend that I am a dealer and we have just reached the end of the shoe. I take the cards out and divide the stack into two equal piles like this. Let's say I have offered the cutting card to you (looking at Steve and passing him the joker to act as the cutting card). Now many dealers do not expect a move to come at this stage of the game because who could possibly cheat during the shuffle?"

"This is where they let their guard down and can become very careless at exposing cards during the shuffle. I have even seen dealers shuffle cards in mid air thinking that this looked good. There are many occasions where the bottom card in their hand is visible as they are about to put the freshly shuffled segments onto the main stack. As the dealer places each shuffled segment onto the main central pile, each segment can leave an identifiable break from which the cutting card can be inserted."

"But what if the dealer squares the cards up?" asked John.

"If they do that then the move cannot be done, but my point is that many dealers fail to spot this and don't think that certain cards can be identified once the shuffle has been completed." I deliberately placed an ace at the bottom of a shuffled segment to illustrate my point. I then placed the segment onto the final stack and, after completing the shuffle, neglected to square them up.

I offered the cards to Steve for him to cut: "Can you see where the breaks in the cards are? Just simply insert the postillion in front of the ace."

After he did so, I put that segment to the back and the cards would have been inserted into the shoe in this order if we had had one with us. To add dramatic effect I said, "First box to the maximum" and proceeded to deal the ace of clubs out as the first card.

Everybody looked on dumbfounded and I said "Do you want to know the good news?" They all stared in silence without replying, "It's not even cheating. Whose fault is it if the dealer hasn't done their job properly?"

"Most dealers won't do that though," remarked John.

"Maybe not," I said. "But you only have to find one for it to make us a lot of money and, believe me, we will find a lot more than one."

All three of them were really starting to buy in to my theories by this stage and my job was starting to get a damn site easier because they were coming up with ideas and suggestions themselves, which is always a good sign. In fact, I had to slow them down a bit because many of their ideas were not workable.

"I like your idea about only going in on poker nights," said Steve.

"Don't misunderstand me, Steve, we can't just go in for poker tournaments because we will not get enough action that way and we don't want to be tied only to playing on certain nights. This is why I want to use floating big players," I replied, and continued, "There's something else that I want to do as well to increase our cover."

"What's that?" asked John.

"I want the big players to play roulette," I said.

"But that's just losing money back to them for no reason," said Kevin.

"It's losing money back, but it's not for no reason," I replied. "Don't forget that the big player is supposed to be a high rolling gambler."

"Yeah, but there are loads of high rollers who just stick to blackjack. There is nothing odd in that," answered Kevin.

"The point is that these high rollers don't have anything to hide like we do, and we cannot afford for them to find out because it is game over if they do. Remember that there are only about 120 to 130 casinos in the entire country and the vast majority of those are made up from four major companies. It wouldn't be that difficult to get barred nationwide. Professional blackjack players and teams do not play roulette and the casinos know this but playing roulette in moderation is part of my cover strategy. If we try to grab every ounce of profit out of this then our shelf life will be lessened considerably. The fact that the big player is also blasting away on roulette to the maximum, or close to it, will reduce any fears or suspicions that they might have."

"What will it cost us?" asked John.

"The house edge on roulette is 2.74 per cent but this halves if you play even chances because of the fact that you get half of the bet back if zero goes in (for American readers, this is single zero roulette). So sticking to even chances puts us at a 1.37 per cent disadvantage. So sticking three hundred quid on red would have an expectation of roughly minus four quid per spin. Doing this two or three times per hour is only costing us ten quid an hour."

"How long have you been thinking all this stuff up?" remarked Steve.

"Too long," I said. "What's more, these big hitters that you know don't have to be blackjack players, either, they could just as easily be roulette players who are now trying their luck over on blackjack. The bottom line is that the casinos know that roulette players lose, so they will not fear that type of gambler. Basically it's all about putting on an act and bullshitting, like I said earlier.

When you put a bet down on roulette, make sure that it gets noticed. Shout something like 'get in there' if the bet goes in. Ask other players at the table what numbers have come out or you could even take the numbers down yourself and flit from roulette to blackjack and vice versa; casinos love system players. It doesn't matter what you do as long as you are masking what is actually happening on blackjack."

"So if we are handing about ten quid an hour back to them, how much will we be making," queried John.

"Well, for a start I would advocate playing more on roulette, at least double the number of spins would still be OK," I said.

"But that's twenty pounds an hour down the drain. That's going to take some getting back," said Kevin.

I looked Kevin straight in the eye and said, "Our hourly rate is almost impossible to calculate but I think it will be in the region of five hundred pounds an hour."

"How have you calculated that?" asked John, looking slightly excited but disbelieving at the same time.

I was just about to answer the question when Steve intervened with, "I thought that you had a program on the laptop that calculated things like earn rates."

"I do but that only calculates earning rates for conventional counting; it's almost useless for working out an hourly rate for what we will be doing," I replied. "For instance how do you go about calculating how many weak dealers we are going to meet?"

John proceeded to repeat his previous question: "So come on, how have you calculated five hundred quid an hour?"

"Well, if we can get a situation where we have a counter on two tables then I think that it is not unreasonable to expect about twenty betting opportunities per hour per table. That makes about forty chances an hour and I want us to be getting about four to five hundred pounds a round down depending in the maximums of that particular casino."

I went on, "At two hundred and fifty pounds per box and two boxes, that's about twenty grand an hour of action. I estimate our return on turnover to be about 4 per cent and that works out at eight hundred an hour. I always like to round down and err on the side of caution with these things so I arrived at about five hundred."

It was about this time that the questions started to get more searching and forceful, but I knew that it was not going to be easy and that I would get a rough ride from these guys sooner or later. "So how can you be sure of getting twenty grand an hour down if you have no data to go on," asked John.

"I didn't say that I had no data," I replied, "Just that there were too many variables to calculate it exactly." I went on, "With conventional counting, the edge is about 1 per cent at best in this country and that's for very skilled counters, which few people are." As soon as I said this I knew that it had come out wrong and this would certainly have upset Kevin and John, although they said nothing.

"The frequency distribution charts that I have at home have helped me to arrive at this figure," I said.

"What are they," asked Steve.

"Basically, they are charts that tell you just how frequently you will encounter situations in blackjack when you have certain levels of edge. If the count indicates that you have a 2 per cent edge for instance, the frequency distribution charts tell you how many betting opportunities will crop up for every hour on average."

"Have you devised these charts yourself?" asked Kevin.

"Good god no!, they were devised by mathematicians far more skilled than me and some of the best blackjack theorists on the planet."

"Anybody we know?" asked John.

"Not unless you study and follow blackjack," I replied. "Remember that we will be placing bets in many situations that card counting would miss. There will be a few situations that we will miss when good situations arise on more than one table at the same time, but there won't be much overlap," I said.

"Is there nothing that we can do on roulette Carl?" questioned Steve. I could tell that Steve was still much more interested with doing a move on roulette – blackjack just didn't seem to be his thing.

"There is but it would mean me being there because it's not something that I could teach anyone," I said. This wasn't strictly true, I was just trying to deter him from moving away from blackjack.

"So what is it then?"

"Academic, anyway, because it's not going to happen," I replied.

"So tell us then," persevered Steve.

"It's to do with block spinning on roulette and detecting non random wheels," I said.

"But the casinos use Huxley wheels and they are supposed to be the best," said John.

"That's right they are, but that still does not prevent bias from happening. Most wheels are not serviced often enough or well enough on a day to day basis. The pit bosses where I worked used a basic spirit level at the start of the shift to level the wheel. Not only was this not enough but the wheels on the other side of the pit were left unsupervised all afternoon during the quiet period and it was not too difficult to get at them," I said.

"But I think that we are starting to get away from the subject here and we should be concentrating on blackjack," I said.

"Could you beat roulette if you had the chance, yes or no?" asked Steve.

"Yes, but tampering with roulette wheels is cheating plain and simple," I said.

"What would they do if they caught anyone?"

"To be honest, Steve, I don't really know but they could make an example of someone by prosecuting them, but I'd be guessing." I smiled and said, "Can we get back to blackjack now? I think that we certainly need to arrange a second meeting. There are still lots of things to iron out before it goes any further."

"Like what?" said Steve.

I went on to list all of the things that we needed to thrash out over the next 30 minutes. Setting all of this up was not going to be easy. For a start, I needed to test Kevin and John's counting and tracking ability. I needed to test their basic strategy as well, all of this stuff couldn't be left to chance. I needed to know that they knew what they said that they knew: could they walk the walk and not just talk the talk.

I was aware that bringing up this subject would be difficult but I didn't give a damn, they may have been counters but they sure as hell had never shuffle tracked, so I had plenty of things to show them. We needed to work out who was putting what amounts of money into this, whether Steve would be financing it all or whether would he expect some kind of financial commitment from the rest of us.

To say that I wasn't rolling in it at the time would be the understatement of the year but I could put a few grand up if need be to show willing. Then we needed to thrash out who would get what as a percentage and what John and Kevin were willing to work for as wages. We also had to work out when we would get paid and who would hold the money. I had to find out the history behind all three of them as well as the big players that we both knew.

Where did they play and for how much? Where were John, Kevin and Steve members and where was it that had barred Kevin? Would we travel together or make our own way there? What dates could we be together? There was countless other stuff that needed to be ironed out. I was a giant step closer to realising my dream but it was all fraught with difficulties. The biggest from my side was the trust aspect: if I was not going to be there in person then I couldn't keep a track on just how much was being won. I could get fleeced by these people but that was a chance that I was willing to take.

"It's getting late," said John, "I've got to be up early for an airport run."

"I want to arrange this meeting as soon as possible, what are you all doing on Sunday?" asked Steve.

As it turned out, Sunday was mutually convenient for us all and I wasn't working so that made it even better. "I would like to make it as early as possible because we have an awful lot to fit in" I said. We agreed on an afternoon appointment back at Steve's place.

"Right" I said, "Before you go, I have some homework for you. I want you to get several decks of cards and practise cutting exactly 26 cards from the back."

They all looked puzzled for a few seconds until John asked why. "Because if we are lucky enough to run into a casino or a game that does not have a cutting card at the back of the pack then we need to be in a position to take advantage of it," I said.

"Come again," said Kevin.

"Remember when I told you the story of the punter who took us to the cleaners on blackjack when we were not using a cutting card to shield the identity of the back card," I said.

"Yeah, but they allowed him to only cut one card and other places won't let that happen," said John.

"Maybe not," I replied, "but if you can cut exactly half a deck then you know that the 26th card out of the shoe will be that card. Let me show you."

I took the cards and put an ace to the back of the stack, deliberately exposing it. "Right, let's say that you manage to see that back card in a real casino as it is being offered to you to cut. If you can cut precisely 26 cards then this portion will be put to the front and you know that the 26th card out of that shoe is an ace."

"Yeah, but what if you miss it by one?" asked John.

"You simply bet three boxes so you are hitting either side of card 26 and this still gives you a huge edge knowing that an ace will go to one of three boxes," I replied.

Steve, looking puzzled, remarked that he couldn't figure out just how we could be certain of the ace arriving on a certain box.

"That's easily explained," I said. "If we have someone like Patty on first base playing two boxes and either John or Kevin playing at the same table, also playing a couple of boxes, it will be easy to just count the number of cards that have been dealt on the first round and then work out just where the ace will fall on the next round. Depending on how many players are at the table, the ace will fall either on the second or third round of play."

I proceeded to deal out an example. I cut the deck precisely on card 26 but of course I had practised like a demon and I could do this blindfolded. The problem that I could foresee was that the casinos would be using cards with different thickness, but a slight adjustment could overcome that.

"That's all very well but what if we never encounter a casino that is this sloppy?" said Kevin, doubtfully.

"Then we will have put in a few hours' work for nothing, but at least we won't get caught with our pants down by failing to prepare," I replied.

Getting the team together

So there it is, the content of our first meeting near as damn it. The conversations have become hazy over the years but this is basically what I showed them and what their reactions were. Driving home, I felt reasonably positive, especially as Steve had said that he would be contacting some of the people that he knew to discuss the idea with them.

I knew full well that there had been an underground network of blackjack players with no money who were always on the lookout for a big player to tag along with. But these guys were assholes, first because they weren't good enough to beat the game and second because they thought that card counting was going to lead to great wealth for them at somebody else's risk and expense.

Card counting is too weak a strategy now, the rules are bad in England and individual counters tend to get caught because of the bet variations, despite some of them using masking techniques like ramping in order to get the money on. The penetration is bad in many casinos for numerous reasons and cutting short shoes is a very effective tactic against conventional counting. My team, if it ever got off the ground, would be different. It would be armed with an arsenal of weapons that any casino would find difficult to combat unless they had shuffling machines. I wanted so much to be a part of it by actually being there because this was how I had always imagined it. But common sense had to take a front seat and my presence would be a serious stumbling block to the potential success of any team.

I had decided not to give the others the details of the software, but was concerned that they may just go it alone without me once they felt that they knew enough. The fact was that they needed me because I understood how casinos work from the other side – though they might not arrive at the same conclusion. I could advise them on where to play and when, and also on when to leave because the heat was on, and the cover may be blown.

I had already mentally prepared a role for Patty and that was first base. She would have numerous uses in this spot but she could also act as a scout and try to get a feel for whether any heat was about to come down. It was vitally important that pit bosses and managers be observed. It was true that they could easily watch us through the CCTV, but most of them won't be that subtle. Time will tell us many things.

CHAPTER 5

THE THEORY OF SHUFFLE TRACKING

I think that it is relatively safe to assume that the vast majority of blackjack players have absolutely no knowledge whatsoever about the dynamics of shuffle tracking. Let's face it, it is rare in England to spot someone who plays accurate basic let alone knows how to count at a professional level or shuffle track. I would also go as far as to say that the proper execution of these techniques has only been performed successfully by a handful of players worldwide.

This is advanced stuff and it is therefore inadvisable for anyone who is not already a highly proficient player to undertake these methods and attempt them inside a real casino environment. When executed well, it is very difficult to spot even for trained personnel. Dealers and supervisors as well as the eye in the sky will be thrown off the scent by the placing of big bets in apparent neutral or negative counts.

It is only correct to point out that the strategy of signalling in a big player even when you are tracking is impossible in many casinos, especially over in the United States. This is because they counter this tactic by not allowing mid-shoe entry. The importance of shuffle tracking and all of the other stuff that you will read about in this book has been accentuated by the fact that tra-

traditional counting is almost becoming obsolete as a method of obtaining any kind of an edge on blackjack.

Even if you are successful, you are maybe looking at a 1 per cent edge at best especially in the UK with its unfavourable rules. This tiny edge makes the financial swings in your bankroll very severe and has been the downfall of many a player. I don't know about you but this is definitely not the type of game that I want to play in; it must have driven some of the earlier counters crazy.

Many casinos have implemented complex shuffles as some kind of safety measure against tracking. They think that this makes them immune but they wrong! Shuffle tracking computer programs that we had could dissect any shuffle irrespective of the complexity, even if it was beyond the skill of the average tracker. It is almost impossible for any human dealer to do a random shuffle because of the time involved in attempting to do it.

Even if they did do substantially longer shuffles, the card information from the previous shoe will still not be diluted totally. You must remember that shuffle tracking is an aid to card counting and not a substitute for it. Most trackers will lose money in the same way that most counters lose money. If this statement shocks you then let me explain.

We live in a world now where everyone seems to be after some quick fix solution. I play professional poker now mainly online but I still teach and coach poker as well as blackjack in my spare time when I am not writing or playing. The overwhelming obstacle that I come across with trying to teach students is their level of impatience and I think that this sums up the human race in general.

We live in a speeded up world where people require everything to be done faster and quicker. Some things just cannot be rushed but when there is a financial incentive, you will be surprised just how many people convince themselves that they know enough and then go out and do their money in. Some of them even come back and claim that what they learnt was wrong.

But I will say it again: the overwhelming majority of blackjack players will fail irrespective of how they attack the game. Failure and success can be measured in many ways but to me, failure is being spotted and prevented from playing by the casino. Going undetected is the true art to blackjack, not the physical act of playing, even if you do happen to be very good. I practised these techniques for literally hundreds upon hundreds of hours, long before I even met my accomplices.

You do not need to practise for as long as I did but there can be no short cuts. I am fully aware that my level of skill is something of a fluke. Blackjack was my hobby and passion for years and the fact that I was a croupier fuelled this into a near obsession. Over the years, I just learnt more and more stuff and got better and better and I was practising inside real casino conditions as well. I realise that everyone else will not have the benefit of that kind of preparation and grounding, but you are going to have to spend a lot of time learning this stuff to become proficient.

Don't get me wrong, using shuffle tracking software will short cut an awful lot of the hard work but I feel that it is still very important to know the mechanics of tracking. This is because the player must still be very accurate in learning the house shuffle and then being skilful enough to spot any minor differences that have been imposed by the dealer.

You need to learn how to break down a shuffle because not all players will have the opportunity to use the software anyway. I will also point out that you do not need to be part of a team in order to shuffle track, but it makes it a lot more effective if you are.

The concept of shuffle tracking is really quite simple. There will always be high card and low card clumps throughout the shoe at various stages. These segments will be dispersed by the shuffle but they will not be eliminated completely. Another advantage of shuffle tracking is the fact that it will soon become apparent when you are making a mistake. This is because the high card clumps should be in a specific area of the shoe if you have tracked them correctly, unlike traditional counting where at the start of the shoe they could be anywhere.

When left to do their stuff without interference, single deck blackjack is the most profitable game for the card counter, but it is the exact opposite with tracking. This is because of the difficulty for the dealer in dispersing the segments with multiple decks. Penetration becomes less problematic for the tracker as well and this is a key issue because it transforms many bad games into beatable ones.

There are so many variations of shuffle that I would literally need to compile an encyclopaedia in order to describe and analyse them all. What is important is that you understand the procedure for breaking them down. Once you understand the process, nearly all shuffles become easy to track.

The basic shuffle types

The vast majority of the casinos use one of the following types of shuffle: the "riffle and re-stack" and the "staggered" shuffle. Many casinos add their own particular variations to them along the way, as will certain individual dealers, and this can confuse the beginning tracker.

The riffle and re-stack shuffle

The riffle and re-stack shuffle will construct a final stack by putting riffled picks from two separate stacks of cards into a third and final pile. This is by far the easiest shuffle to track but it is increasingly rare now outside Europe to see this shuffle. It is basically a five-stage process.

Stage 1

The dealer will take the discards (cards that have already been dealt earlier) and put them onto the table in front of them.

Stage 2

The dealer will then take the cut-offs (cards that are left in the shoe after the final round of play is over) and either place them on the top of the discards or at the bottom. Some dealers insert them into the middle but for the purposes of this example we will assume that they have been topped.

Stage 3

This stack is then usually divided into two equal piles but, once again, there is room here for variation.

Stage 4

Roughly half-deck picks (can vary from dealer to dealer) are taken from each pile and riffled together and then placed separately to begin the formation of the final stack.

Stage 5

The dealer will repeat this process until the initial two piles have been exhausted and the final pile is complete. The dealer will then offer the final stack to the player to be cut.

The staggered shuffle

The other major type of shuffle is called the staggered shuffle, which is more difficult to track than the riffle and re-stack. Do not be disheartened by the apparent complexity of a shuffle, once you have learnt how to do the shuffle as well as a dealer, you can then begin to break it down on paper at home or on shuffle tracking software. The staggered shuffle in its basic form goes like this.

Stage 1

The cards are removed from the shoe (the discards) and placed onto the table in front of the dealer.

Stage 2

The dealer will then take the cut-offs and do exactly the same as in Stage 2 of the riffle and re-stack shuffle.

Stage 3

As in the riffle and re-stack shuffle, the main stack is spilt into two equal piles. This will be two piles of three decks or two piles of two decks depending on whether or not it is a four-deck or a six-deck game (nearly all of the games in England use either four or six decks).

Stage 4

A half-deck pick (can vary from dealer to dealer) is taken from each pile and riffled together to construct a final stack.

Stage 5

Now there is one full deck in the final stack so far. The dealer then takes a half-deck pick from one of the initial two broken piles alternately and shuffles it together with a half-deck pick from the final stack. This is the major difference from a basic riffle and re-stack shuffle.

Stage 6

The dealer will repeat the process until the initial two piles have been exhausted and the final pile is complete. The dealer then offers the final stack to the player in order for them to cut.

Practising shuffle tracking

We have taken a brief look at the two main types of shuffle that are used in casinos. The shuffles can vary from casino to casino and can become almost unrecognisable because of counter measures and dealer quirks and nuances. When I was learning to shuffle track, I used to practise at home with different makes of cards so that I could easily detect where the shuffled cards had gone. The earlier versions of the shuffle tracking software used very similar colour coding.

Once you have identified the weaknesses of a particular shuffle and practised it almost to perfection, then it is time to try it out against a real dealer. A very important factor in shuffle tracking is dealer selection and I cannot emphasise this point enough. The worst dealer to attempt this with is the one who is not consistent with their grab and pick sizes during the shuffle.

Only experience will give you the necessary skills to make accurate visual adjustments with difficult dealers. But I would strongly advise any beginning tracker simply to avoid inconsistent dealers. I advised the players in our team to ignore the entire shoe for tracking purposes unless they were 100 per cent sure that the dealer had shuffled to their normal pattern and they could be certain where the high card clumps were situated.

Making errors with the visual estimations would have led to our big player placing bets in non-positive situations, which would have been disastrous for our bankroll.

How to analyse the shuffle

The vast majority of the work and preparation will be done away from the casino. It must be carried out to a point where, once you enter a casino, the process of actually doing it for real is not that difficult. There are unfortunately no short cuts, only a lot of hard work and practice will get the job done. Luckily for us, most dealers stick to the pattern of shuffling that they have done before or been told or trained to perform.

It would be a great idea at this stage to get several decks of differently coloured cards or cards with different coloured backs and practise various shuffles to see where certain segments get redistributed to after the shuffle. I started out keeping a separate count for every deck that had been dealt from the shoe but I later refined this to every half deck. I used chips to help me keep the individual counts in my head but there are numerous ways that you could do this.

If you know the count for a certain clump of cards and you know where they will be relocated to in the final stack, you can either cut the high card segment to the top or the low card segment to the bottom. Obviously you need to get hold of the cutting card to be able to do this. This is why we used sometimes to have three team members on the same table, but simply asking for the cutting card will suffice as most players tend not to care who cuts so long as they perceive the cutter to be lucky.

Let's say for instance that there has been an unbelievable round of low cards dealt close to the end of the shoe and the running count has jumped from +1 all the way to +12 in one single round of play. Let's also say that there is roughly one deck out of four that is left to be dealt so the "True count" is +12 also. You are licking your lips in anticipation when the dealers reveal the cutting card as they are about to complete their own hand, thus signalling the end of the shoe.

A conventional card counter would be cursing their luck

here, but the shuffle tracker still has an opportunity. This high card segment can be tracked into the next shoe and although it will be dispersed, it will not be eliminated, and if this segment can be married with another high card segment then substantial edges can be obtained in the following shoe.

However, I have said it before, and I will say it again: shuffle tracking is very difficult. If this had been the only weapon that we had at our disposal then I seriously doubt that we would have been as successful as we were. This was because John and Kevin both had quite a bit of trouble picking this up at first. In fact if it were not for the software, I doubt if we would have succeeded at all in this area.

You may say that I took the easy way out by using the software and that this does not make me a pure tracker. Well, say what you like, but I had numerous people putting their faith and money into the decisions that I came up with and these amounts of money were not small, either. It was no good being all macho about this and trying to do it on my own, because if I fucked up early on then I would have lost the confidence of the team, and with it the potential for profit.

Complex shuffles require complex analysis because there are countless variations that can trap the unwary. After all, I was still untried in actual combat so caution was necessary. The team members simply learnt the shuffle of the dealer and relayed that information to me by mobile telephone, usually from the toilet area. Sometimes we would be lucky and get the same dealer almost for the entire night. This happens quite a bit, especially with trainee dealers who are not very proficient on faster games like roulette. The pit boss tends to put them where they can do less harm, which means either chipping up for the dealers or dealing blackjack.

Casino countermeasures and inconsistent dealers can present enormous problems to the amateur tracker but, with hard work and determination, the problems can certainly be overcome. Many casinos now break the cut-offs into several piles and only then insert them into the discards. This procedure makes gaining an edge more difficult because it makes it easier to miss something important. If you have a tendency to lapse into periods of mental laziness after a certain length of time, then shuffle tracking without outside assistance is definitely not for you.

Concentration and keen observation skills are the key, because a slight difference in a dealer grab size and a positive high card segment may not be where you believe it to be. The downside is that no computer program can do this job for you. You need to learn the house shuffle or the shuffle of a particular dealer and then make sure that they are shuffling *exactly* in accordance with what they have done previously.

You need to be vigilant at all times, because even the most consistent of dealers can do something different on a particular shuffle for a variety of reasons. Maybe they are tired or disturbed, or perhaps rushing the shuffle because it is their turn for a break.

What is your edge?

One of the most difficult areas in shuffle tracking is to estimate your edge correctly. There are numerous opinions on this subject and none seem to answer the question properly in my opinion. I am afraid to say that I cannot shed any light on this matter and, not being a mathematician, I couldn't even hope to do it justice even if I tried.

The estimations that I gave to our team members at the initial meeting were just that...an estimation. To be honest I had no idea really how much we would earn, but I knew that we would do well when we dovetailed the other strategies in with tracking. At the end of the day, I couldn't be certain that John and Kevin could carry this out as well as me. I also couldn't be sure of their integrity and of course that applies both ways – although we have a good laugh about this now, as we eventually all became very good friends.

Even if we had a substantial edge, we could have still ended up losing if we had been rumbled during a bad run, although casinos tend only to fear something if they are losing. This was why it was crucial to spread our action and spread it well. So if you were to ask me what extra edge tracking would give you, I would have to answer "I don't know". Shuffle tracking is *potentially* much more powerful than counting when it is done properly, and this is the key word.

Many a counter has come to a sticky end by attempting this stuff and it really should come with some kind of health warning attached to it: *WARNING!! Shuffle tracking can seriously harm your bankroll and state of mind if applied incorrectly*. Although I am not in possession of the relevant data and never will be, it is quite possible that the team earned more from doing the other stuff that we executed than we did from shuffle tracking. This was probably just as well as I couldn't really trust anyone else to do the job as well as I could. This is not big headedness or egotism speaking, it is just that very few people have had my kind of training and practice.

The perils of cluster location

Some wise man (I cannot remember who) once said "Simplicity is the true genius", and this statement applies very well to shuffle tracking. This is why I am going to advise you against getting involved with "cluster location". If you become interested in this subject and decide to take it further by reading other material, then you are likely to come across this by some other name.

Cluster location is the process of tracking tiny, concentrated numbers of high cards and aces and following them through the shuffle and into the next shoe. For example, if there were 20 cards dealt on a certain round of play and 16 of those 20 cards were 10s and aces then this would be a highly concentrated high card cluster. In theory, being able to track these cards successfully may seem a devastating tactic.

If this cluster were to be married with another high card cluster then one can easily imagine the kind of edge that could be obtained…in theory! But reality is a far cry from theory. Now I am sure that there are going to be people out there who will contradict me on this and inform me of their success at this particular strategy. To them I say well done, though just how accurate their reports of success are I really wouldn't like to say.

I do not believe in the validity of cluster location for the simple reason that in my opinion it is far too difficult to get the required dealer consistency. I am also speaking through experience, and costly experience at that. We tried this tactic and failed, despite success at home we were finding it too difficult to execute in the heat of battle. You are basically searching for a dealer who never deviates from their usual pattern for this to work, and that scarcely ever happens.

I am certainly not saying that this could never be done, but when someone who has practised as much as I have is advising you not to do it then I think you had better listen. So if you are contemplating being a tracker sometime in the future then you have a unique opportunity here to save yourself an awful lot of money by learning from our mistakes, or should I say mine, by leaving cluster location at home.

More complex shuffles

Without a doubt, the more casinos that you enter you will eventually run into certain types of shuffle that look incredibly complicated. Multiple pile shuffles are very common now in many casinos and these have to be combated. What I mean by multiple pile shuffle is that when the dealer takes the cut-offs out of the shoe and joins them with the discards, instead of splitting that stack in half, they split it into multiple piles with four being the most common number.

This may look complicated but the shuffle is still perfectly trackable. This is because the dealer is far more likely to grab equal pick sizes because of the smaller piles. For example, if four decks are divided into four piles then it is much more likely that the dealer will take a half-deck pick from one deck and not take a quarter or three-quarter pick. One very important point to remember when selecting dealers is that trainees tend to be far more erratic than experienced dealers and their shuffles can be very difficult to track.

Another thing to point out is that it is just as easy to track a six-deck game as a four-deck one. But casinos tend to use multiple pile shuffles more with six-deck games than four, or at least they have in my experience. Dealers do however tend to be less consistent when only shuffling two piles, although in theory the shuffle should be easier to track. However, this hasn't always been the case in practice for us, as you are about to discover.

Chapter 6

The Second Meeting

Around about the time that I began playing blackjack, I was living with a couple of guys who I had worked with while at the casino. We lived in a three-bedroomed flat overlooking a park, and in summer the view was very pleasant. I had moved in with them under bad circumstances as my marriage had broken up and Paul, the live in landlord and also my workmate, offered me a room, which I was very grateful for at the time.

We were good mates and had some great laughs but we started to drift apart when I left the casino for some strange reason, even though we still lived under the same roof. I have always thought that the guys didn't view me as part of their group any more and saw me as something of an outsider. To make matters worse, Paul had done an awful lot of things that I was not happy with and sometimes there was conflict between us.

Robert on the other hand was a decent kid. He could be a bit selfish but his heart was in the right place. "You off out again Carlos," he said.

"Yeah, I'm meeting Michelle to try and patch things up," I replied. This was a downright lie, we had already broken up and had no chance of getting back together. She had messed me about once too often and I'd had enough of her. I hated lying to Robert because he was a good mate, but telling him the real reason for me going out would have served no useful purpose.

Robert and Paul knew full well about my card counting ability but that was all they knew and I wanted to keep it that way. "You're wasting your time with her," said Robert.

Taking advice from Rob on the subject of women was hardly the best thing to do, especially given his track record. "I know but what can you do? I guess that I'm not that smart with women, Rob. Anyway see you later." I left the flat and headed for the car.

So here we were again, Steve's house take two and this time I was nowhere near as nervous. There were numerous things that had to be ironed out and, to be honest, I didn't expect anything to happen at all. I mean, come on, things like this do not happen to people like me...do they?

I arrived at Steve's house 15 minutes early again and was surprised to see three other cars in the driveway. I knew that one of the cars was Kevin's but didn't know about the other two. I hoped that Steve was not trying to do too much too quickly and attempt to recruit all and sundry. Besides, there was only one person who could do the recruiting and that was yours truly.

As it turned out Steve had been having guests who were just on the verge of leaving when I arrived. I knocked on the door and waited for an answer. To my amazement an absolute stunner of a woman answered the door. "Come on in love," she said, without even asking my name. Turns out that it was Steve's daughter who was just leaving with her boyfriend, who seemed like a real arsehole on first impression. We never had time to get acquainted because she kissed her daddy on the cheek and off they went in her man's brand new Porsche...what an arsehole! That made me feel better – he had a motor that was worth about ten times more than mine.

Steve made the drinks as I made small talk with John and Kevin. I kind of got the impression that they had both been here for a while and I wished I could have been party to the earlier conversation. Steve brought in four cups of coffee on a silver tray, almost dropping them as he had to stride over "Jess", his German Shepherd. Some guard dog she was, I had knocked on the door twice now and she had not barked once.

Steve had insisted on telling me how she was a "killer", but that argument didn't seem to be holding water as she lay on the floor snoring away and breaking wind about every 30 minutes or so.

"Have you been practising cutting half a deck from the back?" I asked no one in particular.

John and Kevin looked at each other in a way that suggested that they had not been doing much in the way of practice.

"So what's on the agenda then?" asked Steve.

"Did you manage to get through to any of your people?" I inquired.

"A couple, but most of them didn't seem interested," he replied.

"How many people have you talked to?"

"Eight."

I was not happy with this situation, Steve seemed to be asking all and sundry and the need for secrecy was obviously not apparent to him. I asked him just what he had been asking these people and how he had approached them, and I was not entirely satisfied with his answers.

But it was difficult for me to be too critical when this guy was contemplating putting a large amount of money at stake, and he obviously wanted to have some kind of control over that. Keeping him in line so this thing might work could prove to be a bit of a problem.

"Before we go any further, I would just like to test John and Kevin's counting and basic," I said. "Do both of you know the high low?"

They both nodded. I proceeded to deal out half a dozen hands on the coffee table and asked them alternately to tell me what the count was. They both answered almost immediately for every round of play that I dealt out. All their answers were quick and correct, which was very encouraging. This was going to short cut a lot of work. If these people had been beginners then I seriously doubt if the entire thing would have got off the ground.

John and Kevin had messed around with playing as a team in the past, but had not been that successful. This was no surprise to me as it needs more than just elementary counting these days to beat blackjack in England. I proceeded to test their basic strategy as well, and this was also spot on.

"Do you need to know the strategy deviations as well?" asked Kevin, just to let me know that he knew them.

"Won't be necessary. It will only over-complicate matters, besides most of them are not that important anyway." I turned to Steve: "If you are going to be a big player, Steve, then I need you to learn basic." I handed him a basic strategy chart that I had printed off the computer.

Steve looked at it as if I had just handed him some highly complex mathematical theorem: "Do I have to learn all this?" he asked.

"I'm afraid so, but it's not as bad as it looks. You will already know most of them and many of the others are just common sense," I assured him. I asked Steve if he had talked it over with Patty and he informed me that he had, and that she was well up for a bit of excitement.

"In that case, Patty needs to learn it as well." I gave him another sheet to give to Patty when she got home from work.

"Why do I need to learn this stuff if I am going to be playing someone else's box?" asked Steve.

"Because we cannot guarantee you being on Kevin or John's box and don't you think that it's going to stand out if every time you approach the table to play, you are always playing with the same player?" I replied. This reply seemed to strike a chord with Steve and he refrained from asking me any more questions about it.

"Right, I need to know every casino where you are a member or have played and how much you have played for. In, short I want to know everyone's entire gaming history."

The contents of that conversation will remain a secret but the reasons that I needed to know this were not immediately apparent to the three of them. It was crucial that we didn't do anything that would be totally out of character from what they had done previously. Casinos keep records of such things and they have very long memories. The key to the entire thing was achieving the necessary results with as much stealth as possible.

"What I am looking to do is to have a pre-designed plan for every casino that we go into," I said.

"I thought that you said that you going in would cause a problem, Carl," replied Kevin.

I told him that I was using the royal "we" to mean the team and not me personally. "I want Patty spotting on first base just playing basic and I want John or Kevin counting at the same table, but not all playing together unless I tell you to, and I don't want too may team members playing on any one night. I want to mix the counters and the big players around so it is more difficult for them to recognise a pattern."

"What about the shuffle tracking?" asked Steve.

"I want you to track the shuffles and then get word to me by mobile. Within a couple of minutes I will get the results back to you," I replied.

"Where do we call you from? Most casinos don't allow mobile phones in the pit," remarked John.

"The toilet is the best place, but you are going to have to be quick because that dealer will be taken off if you are too slow. What we are looking for is consistent dealers who are also weak and prone to errors. If we can find a few of these then that will be the holy grail. I want all team members to be constantly monitoring what is happening with the managers and pit bosses, and I don't mean making it obvious by staring at them, either."

"Yeah, but, we haven't got the experience at spotting these kind of things like you have Carl," said Steve.

"Trust me, you'll know when something is going down. If you see anything that looks dodgy in the pit, then I want you to let me know if you can," I said.

"Like what?" asked John.

"Well things like a change of dealer when they haven't been on the table all that long, for instance." Casinos will change dealers for a variety if reasons – dealers who are losing heavily or too inexperienced for the game will be changed. Usually it is because it is time for them to have a break or maybe because they have to take someone else off for a break. But if the casino is doing it out of fear then that is the time to be wary, because fear causes panic and panic will cause a reaction. That was precisely what we didn't want.

"I also want a debrief after every session before we play the next one. Steve's house is the best place if he doesn't mind, because it is central for all three of us. Do you mind, Steve?"

"Of course not, just give me enough time to get rid of the hookers."

"Don't let Patty hear you say that or she'll have your balls," laughed Kevin.

"They are in her fucking handbag anyway," remarked John, to which we all laughed.

"We are going to have to talk about this eventually, so we may as well talk about it now. What are we going to do about the bankroll?" I asked. To be honest, I still wasn't sure what was going to happen with this and I paused deliberately for a second to give Steve the opportunity to say something.

"You said that one hundred grand could do some serious damage?"

"Yes, maybe fifty would be enough but a hundred would be much better," I replied.

"We were talking about this before you arrived, and we thought that it would be a good idea if we all contributed to the bankroll in some way, even if it is just a token amount," said John.

"Steve's prepared to put up seventy-five grand if we go with a hundred grand and John and I can stump up ten apiece," said Kevin.

I knew from the very beginning that there was a possibility that I would have to find some money from somewhere but I never expected having to find five grand. If I were to say no then I could come across as someone who had absolutely no faith in what it is that they were doing, but five grand: that was close to everything that I had at the time. I obviously couldn't stall on my answer so I quickly replied that I was good for five grand.

"What we thought would be a good idea, Carl, would be if we only played with Steve's money and have ours as a backup. That way we don't have to pass money about all of the time," said John.

"If we get into the hole then we pay Steve at the end of the month our percentage of what we are behind. So if we are ten grand behind at the end of the month, for instance, me and John would pay Steve a grand apiece and you would pay him five hundred quid."

"Sounds good to me" I said. Truth was that I thought it was unlikely that my money would be needed in any great amount. This kind of arrangement put me in total control of my own money because I could effectively pull the plug if things went pear shaped. I know that makes me a bastard but five grand was everything that I had, and I was not going to risk what bit of financial security I had built up for nothing. It was true that because I would be absent from the casino I was placing an awful lot of trust in other people's honesty when it came to them admitting just how much the team won, but that was something that I just couldn't get around, short of playing the game in another part of the world.

"We also thought that any winnings would be divided up at the end of the month," said John.

It was then that something occurred to me. Were these guys thinking that we were going to split the winnings exactly the same way as the losses, because if they were then there was no way that I was working for 5 per cent of the total winnings. Steve may have been putting up 75 per cent of the capital but these guys would be nowhere without me and I was certain that they knew it. I politely and carefully raised the point.

"What we had worked out before you came was that Steve got half and me you and John shared the other 50 per cent equally," said Kevin.

I quickly worked out that it came to roughly 17 per cent each for us three and suddenly the world seemed a much brighter place. "Yeah, that's fine," I said, trying to sound cool as if I had everything worked out. Truth was that I was playing half of it by ear and just trying to fill in the gaps as I went along. What they had actually worked out in my absence sounded pretty good to me.

At least in theory, I was getting 17 per cent of something, without them getting direct access to any of my money, and with someone else taking 100 per cent of the initial risk at the beginning. They had obviously talked about this a great deal in my absence, which was no bad thing really. It showed that they were serious about the project and the fact that they were doing a lot of good analysis for themselves helped to take the pressure off me for a bit.

"To be honest, that is very close to what I had in mind," I continued, which was basically not too far from the truth. "What I want to work on is a plan for when we enter the casino. Remember that we cannot be seen to be together."

After that we got down to discuss everything that I wanted to do. This was the part that I had planned so there was no floundering from me here, because these thoughts had been in my head for years and I knew exactly what we had to do. At least that was the theory, I knew that things would go wrong and go wrong they did. But the rest of our second meeting was all about putting the meat onto the bones so that each team member knew precisely what they had to do.

We organised two more meetings and one full training session with me putting John and Kevin through their paces. Steve and Patty's roles were straightforward, but they still needed to know a few things. It was really starting to take shape and we were all getting more and more excited by the day.

CHAPTER 7

THE MAN WITH THE PLAN

This chapter focuses on the plan that I had outlined and the tactics that I wanted us to use. It is basically a summary of the rest of the second meeting and the subsequent two meetings that we had at Steve's house. I was relieved that we had sorted out the issues with the bankroll without me basically having to do anything. They had come to a conclusion and I was very happy to go along with it.

I was beginning to see the logistical problems of co-ordinating everything – it was not as simple as finding a backer and then just doing it. I had been very lucky so far because my backer and team members basically found me, which is not the normal way of doing this sort of business. But I have to admit that if I had to choose a team then these people were not ideal.

It was useful not having to train John and Kevin basic strategy or the nuances of counting, but this had hidden dangers as well. It meant that they could be handicapped by their own bad habits from previous counting sessions. Also, neither of them had in fact been successful at blackjack (despite the crap that came out of their mouths) and this could possibly have the effect of causing them to lose confidence if things started badly.

They had some success with the over-under, but that was

down to the game being very easy to beat rather than their own skill. It seemed to me that John, especially, was very stuck in his ways, and Kevin seemed something of a maverick type figure to me. The main problems as far as I could see were them successfully employing the proper persona and doing the tracking correctly.

The act

I wanted them to do numerous things while inside the gaming area and the most important was for them to interact with the staff and management, and not to avoid doing this. Everything had to look as natural as possible because this was the only way we would manage to avoid getting rumbled when we started to win. Casinos understand what conventional counter behaviour is; they look for players who concentrate intensely and avoid interaction. They look for players who have big betting spreads and they look for people who act oddly and suspiciously.

I didn't want the big players to start playing maximums straight away and I instructed Steve to buy in for a reduced amount to begin with. This way, if he started out losing then not only would it save us money but it would also look like he was chasing losses when he started doubling up and playing on roulette. This would have the effect of making him look like a gambler who was simply getting carried away.

Counters tend to act in a very robotic and calculating way, mainly because they are concentrating very intensely. This was precisely why we had to use a very easy count like the high-low because more sophisticated counting systems would have created an image that we didn't want to have.

Playing the strategies that I taught them and shuffle tracking meant that the players could actually spend large amounts of time relaxing and talking with anyone and everyone until the crucial shuffling period came along.

There was in fact a serious argument for having John and Kevin on the same table because they could take it in turns to count and track, and this would add deception to our play. When one tracker is doing something else away from the table periodically, this looks as if they are just the recreational type. Also, one could leave and inform me of the shuffle while the other stayed and continued to play and signal in the big player.

The argument against having John and Kevin on the same table was that we really didn't want all four team members in any one casino at the same time. I felt that this would leave a discernable pattern that, once detected, would seriously shorten the lifespan of the team. But I felt that having John and Kevin working in alternate shifts or with a different big player somewhere else was also a viable strategy. Playing too many hours inside the same casino at any one time was out of the question. It would be all too easy to slip into an identifiable pattern by playing too long.

We also needed an excuse to be in the casino because it would look very strange if several people who were all from the same general area arrived at a casino a hundred miles away, having bypassed numerous other casinos along the way. Why would anyone do that? I felt that playing blackjack on the same night as a poker tournament would help our cover, but it would be even better if we timed our entry to coincide with some other casino event or promotion.

Many casinos view poker players as skilled gamblers and skilled gamblers may just know a thing or two about blackjack – this was something that we had to be aware of. I wanted John and Kevin to look confident and at ease, making plenty of eye contact with staff. We talked about this a great deal and I felt initially that John might have trouble in this department.

But the biggest cover of all would be playing another game with a known negative expectation for the player, and playing

that game for sizeable amounts of money. That game was roulette. It was true that we would be handing back a fair amount
of profit, but I felt that we could absorb that quite easily with the
hourly rate that I was expecting from blackjack. It would be very
difficult for any casino to pin us down as professional blackjack
players when the big player was also betting heavy on roulette.

I had instructed Steve to show emotion when winning and
losing because a lack of emotion looks strange, especially if that
person has been noted as the emotional type to begin with. Doing anything that was out of character would look odd. While I
have yet to meet any casino manager or general manager with
advanced knowledge of blackjack (I have met a few who think
that they know), this doesn't prevent them from noticing when
something doesn't look quite right.

The bottom line was that the team was not entering a casino
just as blackjack players, they were also entering as actors and
actresses. I had planned from the very beginning to take this a
stage further by having more than one big player and alternat-
ing the big players with the counters. Casinos pass information
between each other, and even to rival casinos, so using the same
big player would reduce our working life as well.

But the logistics of recruiting this many people were proving
to be a real headache, although Steve himself was doing much
of the initial interview work. What we couldn't do with the
other big players was to have the same set-up with their bankroll as we had with ours, simply because I didn't have another
five grand and had no intention of coughing up any more
money.

I have Steve to thank for this because most of the other big
players were his contacts and it was his persuasive spiel that
convinced them to come on board. As I have already stated, I
was a little concerned about Steve interviewing and talking to
people without asking me first. I felt that our security and cover

were being compromised by not interviewing in a more structured way. I really think that Steve felt that just because he was putting up the lion's share of the money that this gave him the right to do whatever he wanted and to make decisions.

I also wanted known losing big players to be on the team as well. The type of punter who is almost part of the furniture inside a certain casino is ideal. Then when the team goes on a winning streak, the winnings of this player will be tolerated much more readily than they otherwise would be. There are significant numbers of counters and blackjack players who are constantly on the lookout to tag along with a big player.

But on a darker note, there are also numerous scam merchants who claim to be professional blackjack players. There have been examples of wealthy big players being seduced by someone who could talk the talk. What these people have done is basically to "free roll" with the big player's money. If they start off winning heavily then they take their cut and if things go badly then they simply disappear. They tend to use some worthless doubling up progression type system, which will likely generate a few early wins before the inevitable losses appear.

Getting back onto the subject of Steve, I cannot be overly critical of him as the man obviously wanted more of a say in what happened to his own money and I cannot really blame him for that. Another cover play that I wanted Steve and the other big players to use was to befriend other blackjack players at the table who were not part of the team. If we were successful in this, then every time the big player approached the table, it would look to the pit staff as if they were just coming over to check on a friend and not that they had been signalled in.

I thought that the roulette play would be great cover by itself, but I didn't want to take any chances. This was the idea behind all of the numerous different types of cover plays that I have just mentioned. What I had been trying to do for some time, but without success, was to devise a way to keep our winnings a secret during the actual session of play.

Casino inspectors keep a tally of what certain players buy in for and pass this information on to the pit boss, who in turn passes it on to the duty manager. This can be concealed to a certain extent for average counters but I didn't see how we could conceal anything when the big player would be playing table maximum or close to it. This would really sharpen them up when big chip action was happening. They also do a chip count at the end of the shift, which meant that we couldn't easily conceal our win by hiding chips and then bringing them back in at a later date. I couldn't see an easy way around this, which was why the other cover tactics were going to be very important.

This was the idea behind using numerous big players because, this way, the same person wouldn't be the one who was winning the money. I was concerned that we didn't have enough counters. If John and Kevin were to get rumbled then we were going to be in trouble from a tracking point of view. This was precisely why I wanted to hit the casinos with a battery of tactics, of which shuffle tracking was only one.

It meant that if John and Kevin were unable to continue for any reason then our operation wouldn't have to come to an end. In fact, as I stated earlier, it was possible that the biggest part of our profit (presuming that there was going to be any) could actually come from non-tracking tactics. Spotting weak dealers didn't require anywhere near as much skill but could be far more destructive.

Another major advantage to attacking blackjack with non-card-counting strategies is when you come up against certain members of staff who can actually count. In all my years in the gaming industry, I only ever came across two other croupiers who possessed counting knowledge. These two were a couple whose previous gaming experience had been in South Africa. It was no surprise to learn that they didn't pick this up in England.

Their knowledge was pretty basic and they wouldn't have made it as blackjack players, but that doesn't mean to say that they couldn't spot another counter if they saw one. The pit bosses and managers probably have some basic knowledge as well – I am sure that they must be told this on one of their management courses. But the same applies here: I am still waiting to meet a gaming manager with advanced knowledge in blackjack although I have a feeling that this may change if the contents of this book ever reach certain circles.

If a dealer or manager counted the cards out of curiosity to try and catch us out, our strategies would have totally thrown them off the scent. They could have stood there and counted all fucking day and it wouldn't have done them any good. They would have had to start at the beginning of the shoe anyway, and the big player betting big off the top would have totally thrown them. But I personally believed that our cover was so good that it would never have even come down to this anyway.

I had also placed myself on standby just in case John or Kevin received any heat. It was perfectly possible that I could actually go undetected, especially if I didn't go too close to home. I would have to get someone else to sign me in because joining and becoming a member myself would present them with too much information about me. We are in a computer age now and it really wouldn't be all that difficult for a casino to find out if someone was ex-gaming. This is especially the case when you have to wait 24 hours after you apply before you can enter.

If I could get access by being signed in by someone else then it wouldn't be too difficult to conceal my identity. I don't mean wearing wigs and false moustaches or anything stupid like that, but there are numerous ways that a person can dramatically alter their appearance without doing anything too drastic. But that was in the event of an emergency, because the risk of being identified was too great in my opinion. If I was ever spotted and associated with these people then we really wouldn't be aware that anything was going off until it was too late. I had designed our covert tactics in such a way that the big players were going to look like gamblers and of course, in several instances, they actually were.

The weapons

First base man

This was a job that I had designed for Patty. The first box on a blackjack table is known as first base but the last box (third base) has always historically been known as the "counter's box." It is on first base that a player is in a perfect position to spot the first card of the next round of play if a dealer is careless enough to expose it.

When I say expose, what I actually mean is to make the card fractionally visible to the player at first base. Fast dealers are far more likely to do something like this than slow ones. Trainee dealers do have trouble adding up hand totals early in their careers, but they tend to deal so slowly that the inspector usually prevents them from pulling another card to their own hand when they already have a total to stand on.

There is a name for this – "faster than eye action". This basically means dealing faster than your brain can add up the total. It is also perfectly possible to manipulate this kind of error even more by commenting on the dealer's impressive speed and professionalism. Massaging the ego of certain dealers just increases their desire to show off even more by dealing even faster. This is perfect because it also increases the chance of dealer error.

When a dealer makes an error that is capitalised upon, the staff basically shrug their shoulders and let it go. Their mindset is that the money will eventually come back because the people who frequent these places are gamblers and gamblers are inherent losers. But the fact of the matter is that when you are playing accurate basic strategy, the player is only at a disadvantage of about 0.5 per cent. This means that the dealer really cannot afford to make any mistakes at all.

It is precisely this philosophy that underpins the strategy used to defeat blackjack games with shuffling machines, because the weakness of the game is the human element and the human element is the dealer. The kind of mistakes that dealers make are numerous, and this is why blackjack can be beaten without counting or tracking. Dealing the cards too quickly for their own skill level is one weakness; handling the cards incorrectly is another.

Many dealers exert too much pressure on the cards as they deal them and this leads to all kinds of problems. While the cards were changed on Caribbean Stud Poker every hour, they were left all night on blackjack and never changed. Many of the cards were bent and just because they were in a shoe, I thought that the casino staff believed that this made them safe.

Most dealers basically don't give a damn if they do the entire float in, despite the front that they put on. They care even less about little things like slightly warped cards. From their point of view, nothing ever happens from shift to shift, and they simply lower their guard. This is especially the case towards the end of a nightshift when staff begin to get really jaded.

It is actually possible to increase your skill at spotting flashed cards. Dealers believe that they deal the cards so fast that it is impossible for anyone to see anything tangible. This is blatantly wrong. There have been cases where some players have trained themselves to spot flashed cards by using devices like tachistoscopes to improve their visual awareness.

We didn't have access to that kind of equipment but there is a very useful practice technique that when done properly has a very similar effect. You simply take a deck of cards and ask a partner to select a card, without telling you what it is, turn it the other way around and place it back in the deck. Your partner then runs his thumb across the top of the cards with enough pressure to slightly bend the deck as they fan them and this must be done very quickly.

The target is to identify what the reversed card is. At first it seems impossible but it is surprising how your eyes adjust to the speed. After a while you will begin to see the card – it is a bit like staring at one of those pictures where you have to look at them for a certain length of time before the image appears. I had practised this for several years and I became very good at it. I wanted every team member to practise it as well.

The main reasons were because the shuffle tracking can be a very difficult thing to do, especially inside a live casino environment. If we only had this as part of our arsenal and John and Kevin started having difficulties then our operation was going to come to a very quick and sad conclusion.

Whoever was playing first base would then simply stall the dealer, while the big player was subtly signalled in. Depending on the position of the table, first base could also be an ideal spot to observe the pit area and watch for potential heat.

Scout man

I didn't just want to enter a casino without having done some homework on that particular club. I wanted to know in advance what the house shuffle was or whether dealers basically did their own thing. I wanted to know things like dealer competency and table placement relative to the CCTV cameras and the pit desk.

This was a job that I could do, because even if I were to be spotted I wouldn't actually be doing anything on that particular evening. Once I had trained the others, then this was something

that they could do themselves as well, but at the outset it probably had to be me.

I would be able to get a feel for the place after a very short
space of time. I could estimate their average action, which
would have given me an idea of just what kind of bet levels
would have unnerved them. I didn't want to go into some
crummy shit hole where the management started having kittens
because our big player put more than a hundred quid on a box.

Proper scouting would mean that we would never enter a casino blind and I could even start building my dealer dossiers
while I was there.

Damaged cards

When I had been in gaming, I had always felt that one of the areas where the casino was vulnerable was when cards became
damaged on blackjack. Some of the punters were very rough
and forceful when they cut the deck and the cutting card would
sometimes be damaged or even torn. The procedure was then to
take that card out of play and the game was held up until the
replacement card was brought back.

If this were to happen towards the end of the shift, the replacement card wouldn't look quite the same as the others on
the outside edge. It would be subtly brighter in colour than the
rest of the cards and it was cleaner because it had been taken
from a sealed, unused deck. The difference in shade was very
subtle, but it could be identified once you knew what to look
for.

Despite the fact that you still couldn't identify it in the shoe,
you could identify it while the dealer was shuffling. If this card
happened to be an ace or a 10, then identifying that card and
cutting it to the front would have guaranteed that this card
would be the first card out of the shoe.

This leads us into a very murky area, one where this event

could actually be manipulated. If a team member were to get hold of the cutting card and deliberately damage the edge of it, this would then have the effect of damaging a card when it was inserted into the stack without having to use the same amount of force. Then it is down to luck if the damaged card is an ace or a 10. But if it was, and bear in mind that it will be one of these cards precisely four times out of 13 on average, then potential big profits could be realised between now and the end of the shift.

I must point out that this was not something that I instructed our team to do, I wanted to beat them and I wanted to beat them bad, but I also wanted to do it legally and skilfully, and not by doing some cheap trick. Plus, if we were ever to get caught then there could have been legal repercussions from trying to pull this kind of stroke. I wanted us to take advantage of this opportunity if it ever presented itself, but I didn't want us to manufacture it.

There is actually another marvellous cheating technique that once practised and perfected can be very destructive. Once again, we never used it because I was the only one of us who could do it to the required standard and we didn't have the time for the others to put in the required amount of practice anyway.

This tactic is to twist the cutting card slightly on inserting it into the stack when you are cutting. The twist exposes a card in the middle of the stack; the player retracts the cutting card as if they are not happy with the cut and re-inserts it back into the stack, but this time in front of the card that has been exposed if it is a 10 or an ace. This card will once again become the first card out of the shoe.

This sounds much easier in print than it is in practice and the double cut must be almost one movement to make it look totally natural. Neither John or Kevin would be able to come anywhere near the level of skill required in order for it to look innocent. I have included these techniques merely to illustrate what can be achieved on a blackjack table. But once again I must reiterate that this was not something that we undertook to do.

Flashed cards

I wish that I had £100 in my pocket for every dealer who believes that they are the best dealer on the planet. Many dealers believe that just because they can deal the game fast, this somehow qualifies them to be labelled as good, but they do so from the same base as the many poker players who over-estimate their level of skill. They over-estimate their skill because they have had success, but this success – if you can call it that – has been in small home games where their opposition has played even more poorly than they have. Just because they end up winning a bit of money in this game, suddenly they think that they are Doyle Brunson.

It is the same with dealers. Their mistakes go unpunished by clueless punters so their errors never get highlighted. Any dealer who over-estimates their own skill, becomes tired, bored, fed up and so on is a target for the professional. Many dealers shuffle carelessly; they simply will not believe that they are under any kind of a threat at this stage of the game. Sloppy dealers when shuffling two piles of cards together regularly expose cards to an alert player.

I have worked with experienced dealers who actually held the cards several inches off the surface of the table in the belief that they were doing something clever. They then place the cards on top of the other shuffled cards without any care whatsoever. What they fail to notice is the natural break in the cards when they do this. Do not take my word for this, try it. Take several decks of cards and shuffle several stacks together and place each stack on the top of each other.

You will notice how easy it can be to spot each break in the cards and if you happen to have seen what the bottom card was of a certain segment, then this card can be cut to the top and become the first card out of the shoe. I have seen and worked with dealers who were so sloppy that they never even bothered to square the cards up before offering them to be cut. Is it any wonder that casinos lose money to professionals when they have dealers who behave like this? Nearly every single dealer has some sort of bad habit. They tend to manifest themselves early on in the dealer's career.

Half-deck cutting

I have already mentioned this tactic and it was something that I certainly wanted us to have in our arsenal if we were ever presented with an opportunity. Some casino blackjack games have been known not to use a cutting card at the back of the stack when shuffling up. I know this for a fact because I have worked in one. This means that the back card can be visible to one of the players, depending on how the dealer holds the cards.

Even if the dealer uses a cutting card, it is still possible for a careless dealer to expose the back card. If you can acquire the skill of being able to cut a certain number of cards from the back then it is certainly possible to direct the back card to a certain location on the second round of play. The reason that I stated the second round and not the first of the third is because most casinos have a rule that forbids a player to cut any less than half a deck from the edge, and 26 cards tend to fall on the second round of play in an evening game in England.

A table that had Patty and another team member on it would be in an ideal situation to guide the card onto a certain box. In fact this would be a serious argument for having John and Kevin operating at the same time. If there weren't many players at the table then the card could appear on a later round, possibly the third. Being able to cut precisely half a deck is not that difficult and can be mastered with a bit of practice. I was not convinced that our team members would have that accuracy so I instructed them to go one card either side with their estimation and the big player was to play card number 25, 26 and 27.

I had always felt that John was not very comfortable in doing this because it placed him under too much pressure. It would be apparent to everyone if he made a mistake because the 10 or the ace wouldn't be where he said that it was and he couldn't cover up his error to the team. In our debriefs I found out that the team had never executed this tactic. This meant that we were either unlucky or they were just too afraid to try the move.

I always felt that this was a shame because the edge that can be obtained when you know that a certain card is going to land on a certain box (namely an ace or a 10) is huge in gambling terms. It is over 50 per cent for an ace and about 13 per cent for a 10-value card. Even if we divided this edge by playing three boxes, this would still have meant a very profitable situation for the team.

But I would rather the players admitted that they were not up to doing something than trying to be macho about it and costing the team a lot of money, or should I say costing Steve or the other big players a lot of money.

Shuffle tracking

Here we come to the main part of our strategy or at least I thought that it was the main part at the time. It had been my belief that shuffle tracking would provide the bulk of our hoped for winnings and that it would be these strategies that would basically underpin everything else.

I knew that if John and Kevin were successful with the tracking then they could simply pass on the data to me by mobile phone and I could get the relocation of the high segments back to them within a couple of minutes. I had warned them to turn their phones off until the time came for them to call me, as we couldn't afford for their phones to go off in the middle of the pit area. Mobile phones were not permitted in many casinos back then and most players were told to leave them on reception. I would be doing the scouting anyway, so I would have a very good idea of just what kind of shuffles each casino were implementing.

Despite this, there was huge scope for a colossal cock-up as the real skill to tracking is in spotting and identifying the subtle differences in the shuffle. These differences would run contrary to the information that I had and was inputting into the tracking software. I had severe reservations that John and Kevin could successfully pull this off. I was certainly not getting good vibes from them during the course of the training sessions.

I had instructed them in what I thought was the best way to count individual segments and how to store that information at the table. I had contemplated just asking them to play for the cut-offs, but that seemed like too weak a strategy to me. I knew that we would make money exploiting weak dealers but I was afraid that this may be wasted by John and Kevin getting the tracking wrong in a big way.

One of our problems was that because it was next to impossible to measure our expectation, I couldn't estimate our standard deviation, either. In a nutshell, what this meant was that John and Kevin could have been fucking up big time and I wouldn't know for certain until it was too late whether it was mathematically normal or whether something serious was amiss. To be honest, even if by some miracle we could have accurately measured our expected earning rate, I would have been amazed if we would have achieved any more than 50 per cent of it anyway.

CHAPTER 8

KEEPING UP THE STANDARDS

I can honestly say that when our operation was completed, there had never been one single occasion in which we had cheated. All of the plays that I have described involve mistakes on behalf of dealers and skill on our part. I was proud of that fact and I still am to this day. As new people came on board, it became far more difficult to keep track of what everyone was doing and some of them wanted to do their own thing and had their own ideas about how it should be done.

We were doing fine for about 18 months and then the real arguments started. First it was about tactics, later about money and who should get what and when. I had tried to stay out of this for as long as I could but Kevin had accused me of not earning my money because I was working from home and they were the ones who were at the sharp end. He seemed to forget the fact that it was I who had done the scouting and it was my expertise that had got this thing off the ground, coupled with Steve's money.

I had always known that I would have trouble with Kevin. At times it was an absolute nightmare trying to get him to put the time in. If it wasn't for me he would have been past posting on roulette and would have had his arse handed to him on a plate by now. But Steve and Kevin were always trying to drag us into areas that I didn't want to go into. Steve knew full well how much more successful we could be if we colluded with dealers and inspectors. I knew perfectly well how to approach staff in and out of work and Steve knew this. Staff are always getting approached by dodgy punters and numerous stories of the gaming underworld reach my ears from the grapevine.

I knew that a poker dealer and a cocktail waitress had been in collusion with a player a few years back. The waitress would bring over the drinks and would openly flirt and make sexual innuendos to the players. She was very pretty by all accounts, so getting their attention was not too difficult. On passing a drink to the dealer, she also placed a stacked deck in their lap which was easy to switch into the game as she continued her show. The player whose turn it was to choose the poker variation would simply choose Hold'em or whatever coincided with how the deck was stacked.

The strength of this play is that no one at the table would suspect a dealer or a cocktail waitress of cheating and would never look for it. The casinos are very vulnerable to collusion and they know it. For instance imagine how powerful it would be if a dealer actually did the counting for a big player and then signalled them in. Taking this a step further, the dealer could even manipulate the shuffle if need be and keep high card clumps together. The only problem with this is that the dealer could go for long periods of time without dealing blackjack. Although I have worked with soft pit bosses who have let the dealer go where they wanted if that dealer were to ask politely.

Even in clubs that have CCTV there are countless moves that can be done in the open that CCTV would be useless to detect. For instance there is a well-documented move on roulette where a trainee dealer accepts a call bet just before the ball is about to drop. The punter fires a series of numbers at the trainee knowing full well that they are not going to remember them. The inspector is colluding with the punter and as the ball drops into the number, the punter lets out a scream of joy as if to say that the ball has landed in their number.

It is the procedure (or was in certain clubs) that if the dealer has time to place a bet then they must do it. But if they haven't then it goes on the wheel. The inspector instructs the dealer to put the bet onto the number even if it has lost. The trainee dealer either does not have the ability to remember the bet or the nerve to question their supervisor. Unless a casino has audio surveillance as well as visual surveillance then this move cannot be picked up on CCTV. There are countless others.

A common cheating method with this technique is for the punter to say a number with its neighbours that sounds like another number. For instance if they said "Seven and the neighbours by fifty pound" they then claim that they actually said "Eleven and the neighbours by fifty pound." This is cheating plain and simple, and I wanted no part of it. Truth was that Steve was reticent about risking large chunks of money and I cannot blame him for that.

This was why he was shocked with a return on investment of only 5 per cent. He wanted to walk into a casino and never have a losing bet. The only way that this can be achieved is by cheating but any fool can cheat, although I have to admit that to cheat well takes great skill. Steve was constantly on at me to divulge cheating methods on roulette and I refrained from telling him. The reason I did this was because I knew full well that they would go down this route once they had the knowledge and would very quickly be playing behind my back doing something that we had not worked or agreed on.

Steve told me that he had heard of a team who had won thousands past posting on roulette. I basically told him not to believe all of the stuff that he heard or read because most of it was crap. Even if you could get away with such a manoeuvre, the team would have a very short working life.

If you are contemplating trying to beat the casinos or any other gambling establishment then you have really got to understand your enemy and this principle applies to many things. It applies to warfare and business very strongly and even to games like poker. If we assume in this case that our enemy is the casino, then we have to understand their strengths and weaknesses and not just attempt to go at it like a bull in a china shop.

In the end these people are professionals with an awful lot of experience and knowledge of the industry that they are in, and that fact must be respected. The way to beat them is by preparation and imagination and not just by charging in.

For instance during one of my scouting sessions, I came across a casino that had an upstairs restaurant and bar area that was separate from the actual gaming floor. It was impossible to see the gaming tables but I was still card counting while having a drink at the bar. If I couldn't see the tables then how could I possibly count the cards? Well, situated over the bar were several television screens that were showing the action from the gaming tables downstairs.

This was obviously an attempt by the casino to attract non-gaming customers onto the tables downstairs. The TV picture was crystal clear, I could see everything. It was at that moment that an idea hit me; I thought how good it would be to have a counter in the upstairs bar and a big player downstairs. We could secretly signal in the big player by using silent vibrating mobile phones. The big player downstairs would feel his mobile activate inside his trouser pocket and know that this was a signal for him to approach the table and play.

A second signal would indicate that the count had gone negative and this meant that they had to move away from the table. If there was more than one table open then we could use more than one phone – it was that simple. There was only one remaining question that had to be answered: were these pictures accurate and, above all, live?

That question had been answered after only five more minutes. I had asked my partner Angela if she minded going downstairs and walking up to the blackjack table. I then instructed her to thrust her arm out over the table as if she was pointing to something. Obviously if she was going to do this then she had to ask a question of some sort which would give her a reason for the action.

I asked her what time she had on her watch and our watches were exactly 35 seconds apart. I told her to look at her watch just before she did it and record the time. The action on the upstairs TV was real time and not recorded. I thought that this idea was brilliant and so did Angela. I would like to report a very happy ending to this story, but unfortunately when we tried it out for real we were struggling to get a signal inside the building, and sending phone calls within the building by mobile was proving to be impossible.

We tried different phones with the same result, but I am sure that six years on, with better mobile phone technology, this could now be achieved. I have told this little story just to give an example of beating the casinos by imagination.

I also knew that the tactic of dealers exposing cards could also be exploited on Caribbean Stud Poker as well. There are certain casinos that had CSP tables where the dealer sat down to deal the game but there were others where the dealer stood up to deal the game. There doesn't seem to be a great deal of importance here, but if you can imagine a small dealer on a table where the table top is at stomach level, then you do not need to have much imagination to see that this dealer will more than likely be exposing cards.

I don't mind exploiting this type of error because it takes a lot more skill than you might imagine to see flashed cards, be it on CSP or blackjack. I knew that I could have beaten roulette in numerous different ways as well, both skilfully and by cheating. But roulette never carried the fascination that blackjack did for some reason. Maybe I just wanted to emulate Edward Thorp, Ken Uston and all the rest of my blackjack heroes.

The way to beat roulette is obviously not with mathematical systems in the traditional sense. Mathematicians the world over have proved this over the years, so who was I to question them. The odds that are built into the game are what defeats system players, that and the maximums. But it is those same odds that are the game's biggest weakness when it is attacked in a different way. I really do not want to go into that within the confines of this book because it would be straying too far from the track of what is important here – blackjack.

After that initial 18-month period, it became increasingly difficult for me to keep discipline within the team. I know for a fact that Kevin was off doing his own thing because of reports that I was getting back. Some of the things that he was doing certainly were not with my blessing, but what could I do?

I was really paying the price for not getting my own people in but I couldn't complain too much because I was basically on a free roll with someone else's money. I was not fooling myself, this little venture would probably never have happened had it not been for Steve's financial input. The three of them certainly had the nerve to do something daring but they were very green and constantly had to be refrained from doing anything stupid. Steve was seduced with cheating moves and other shady stuff, but this kind of approach could have had severe repercussions not just for him but for us as well.

Towards the end of 2001, the team had certainly lost its discipline and it became something of a farce, which I still find sad even to this day. I have had many highs and lows in my life but the break up of that team was a definite low point for me. I found out some while later that Steve and two of his companions from down south had took "substantial" amounts of money off roulette. This was always the way that Steve had wanted to go and I was not in the least bit surprised.

Was I sad to miss out on all of this profit? Well, I remember thinking at the time that I could have done with the money but it takes balls to cheat the way that they did inside a casino. I had always fought against telling Steve what I really knew about roulette. But over the space of 18 months I think that he had built up a dossier from all of the bits and pieces that I had told him along the way.

The biggest worry regarding the break up of the team was my loss of income, but I knew that there was always a job back at the casino waiting for me, because I was certain that no one from the gaming industry knew who I was, although I have never put this to the test.

A couple of times my cover had been nearly blown even before I left the gaming industry. At one time the assistant general manager came to live with me and my two flat mates for about three weeks after he and his wife split up. One evening when my two friends were working the night shift, the AGM and I decided to go into town for a few drinks as we were decent mates. I think that he appreciated the fact that I understood his position and I never placed him in an awkward situation.

We came back in the small hours much the worse for wear, having downed one too many drinks, and I recalled the next morning that I had shown him sensitive blackjack material as well as blackjack software on my computer. It seemed harmless at the time, especially with about ten bottles of Bud inside me. At this stage I never thought that this knowledge would actually go anywhere. I must confess that the reason that I did this was mainly out of ego. I wanted to show him how intelligent and clever I was for knowing this stuff and that I could teach my superiors a thing or two about blackjack.

Looking back, it was stupidity of the highest order and I cannot believe to this day that I actually did that. Luckily for me, I don't believe that the AGM took me too seriously and probably presumed that it was nothing more than a member of staff having an intense interest in their job, although I think that he knew me better than that.

The second incident occurred close to when I was leaving the industry for good. This was when I had a full blown argument with a duty manager who was an ex-general manager in the middle of the pit area. One of the blackjack tables that I had been inspecting dipped a large amount of money (large by our standards but not in the real world). I had been having a conversation earlier in the evening with this manager about the relative inexperience and lack of skill with the current staff.

I could have been rude during this conversation, by saying that if staff were treated right and paid right then experienced staff wouldn't leave and there would be no need for constant training schools. In my opinion this was the main reason why the average skill level in the pit was low.

A known female punter and perhaps the largest female punter that we had at the time won a sizeable amount of money on the table that I was watching. It was entirely normal: her play was terrible, her basic strategy almost non-existent. She just did what countless other bad players do from time to time and got lucky. She quickly emptied a couple of chip trays; then for some reason I was taken off the table and replaced. This manager made a comment as he walked past me: "See what I mean about crap staff." As he walked off, I realised that he meant me.

As I entered the roped-off area of the roulette pit I walked up to him and asked him to explain his remark. Everyone was afraid of this manager, who was very aggressive when things were not going well in the pit. On top of that he was without a doubt the most unprofessional manager I have ever worked with and I couldn't believe that this guy had ever got to be general manager.

"Why didn't you tell the dealer to start cutting short shoes?" he blurted out.

"What's the point in that?" I replied. At this stage, I knew that I was close to leaving and I was ready for a confrontation with this guy. The same guy who would go up to a roulette table that was losing money, put his hand in the wheel and physically speed it up himself to a pace where the ball would fly out of the wheel or take forever to come to rest in a number.

He was intensely paranoid about roulette and I cannot blame him for that because he knew as well as I did just how vulnerable the game was. But the only person who should have done this at all should have been the dealer. For anyone else to do it looks bad and grossly unprofessional. "What do you mean, what's the point? Do you need me to tell you why after all this time?" he asked.

We had a procedure of cutting short shoes whenever a blackjack table was losing heavily, which was one of the stupidest things I had ever come across. This just underlined how staff and even management didn't understand the game or the mathematics inherent in it. There is only one reason purposely and strategically to cut a short shoe (deal less cards out than what is normal), and that is to thwart a card counter.

This tactic prevents them from getting too deep into the shoe, where the greatest advantages lay. But to do it just because a table was losing to a bad player was crazy and counterproductive. I asked him in reply, "Would you tell a roulette dealer who was losing money to slow their game down?"

"Of course I wouldn't, what's that got to fucking do with it." He would often swear at staff and that was not all, I had heard him make disparaging remarks about certain members of staff to other staff, which I cannot repeat because they are of a personal nature. He would curse and swear in front of punters whenever the pit or a certain table started losing money.

To be honest, the guy was something of a joke and was the gaming industry's answer to Basil Fawlty. He retired shortly after I left, but that was years too late as he was nothing but a dinosaur and had been for ages.

"What it's got to do with it is because that is exactly what you are doing on blackjack," I replied. This was perfectly true because increased shuffling time because of shorter shoes can only serve to slow the game down and this was just crazy.

They had obviously heard of some anti-card-counting strategy and then started to use it in totally the wrong situation and no other member of staff had the knowledge to correct this, so it just became policy over the years.

He countered with, "When a table is losing with 30 minutes of the shift left then the result has got to be protected."

I tried in vain to show him the error in this thinking, because it is all one long shift after all, and it would all start again in 10 hours' time when the afternoon shift started.

To cut a long story short, I ended up saying far too much and I was lucky to get away with it. "Look Carl, I am aware that you know stuff about blackjack but, trust me, you don't know what you think you know." There was no point in arguing with the man but that didn't stop me at the time. I vividly recall every member of staff turning around to find out what all the commotion was about, and the shock on their faces when they saw the two of us verbally slugging it out in the middle of the pit.

At that point I didn't care that he knew about me knowing certain things about the game. What he didn't know was the other stuff that I knew on top, which would have made me public enemy number one in their eyes. Managers in England prefer to keep their staff in the dark about such things as advantage play on roulette and blackjack. They basically tell them what they need to know and no more than that.

There are ways to beat roulette but the best ones I only discovered after I left gaming, funnily enough. But once again I had been served a warning that the management knew about my blackjack knowledge. Of course I only had myself to blame for this. I was not sure about their procedure for keeping records but I wouldn't have been surprised to find my name on a database of undesirables. I knew that casinos kept records of members who were barred and for what reason, and they keep these records a very long time.

An acquaintance of mine who was barred for counting from a previous casino where I worked is still barred to this day from that club. It is so simple now to process and pass detailed information and every casino takes your picture these days when you become a member or are signed in. I am sure that there must be some UK version of the "Griffin Book" that all casinos have access to. After all, it is in their own best interests to share this information even from company to company. Every casino shares a common goal of protecting themselves from counters, cheats, advantage players, ex-staff and generally anyone who happens to know too much.

This was precisely the reason why I couldn't actively be part of a team. True, I could have altered my identity and I am confident that I stood a good chance of pulling this off, but what was the point in taking the risk? The only valid reason for me doing this was if John or Kevin were proving totally inadequate with the tracking and the advantage play.

CHAPTER 9

MERRY CHRISTMAS, MR SAMPSON

December 1998

I really hated Christmas; they never seemed the same after my divorce. I really missed my young daughter as well at this time of year. We would see each other quite often but it never felt the same as being with her all of the time. Walking round the Meadowhall indoor shopping centre was not my favourite pastime and shopping was not my favourite pastime, either.

I would get very jealous and envious when I saw happy couples because this reminded me that I was on my own and had no one special. It wasn't until the following July that I would meet Angela. I had a massive void in my life and I needed to fill it or it would send me crazy. Spending nights on my own seemed strange, I was not used to being on my own and although I had two flat mates, they were still at the casino working nights.

I had got into the habit of leaving the television on purely for background noise and hated going to bed because this meant being in bed on my own. I needed to get out of the flat and fast. There were too many things flying through my head when everything was quiet and there was no distraction. I needed to do something, my new career was starting to bum big style and I really didn't want to admit defeat by crawling back to the casino begging for a job with my tail between my legs. That would have been the ultimate insult.

It was definitely time for some positives in my life because there had not been many lately. In a way, I needed blackjack like a bird needs wings. That brings me on to another point – that I would probably not have pursued this venture if my life had been filled with happiness and focus.

But my life had drifted and I was stagnating. I was fed up with not achieving anything. I had left school without meaning-ful qualifications not because I was stupid – I was probably the smartest kid out of the 1,500 that were there – but because I had lost focus during those final, crucial couple of years.

I hated the fact that people who were less intelligent than I were my superiors and earning more money than I was, but who was to blame for that? I was desperate in many ways: here I was at 30 years of age with no decent job or income, no partner and no focus. I was grasping at something when I undertook this caper with the boys, because there was just no way that I would have put money at risk otherwise, because I was just too cautious.

So here I was doing some Christmas shopping for my little girl. I was almost done and a quick glance at my watch told me that I didn't have long before I would be setting out on my first scouting mission. I had joined a few casinos and become a member, but I knew loads of people who could sign me into others as well. I was about done with the shopping for another Christmas, thank god.

The girl at the checkout took my money with the kind of look on her faced that suggested that she wished that she was some-where else. I knew the feeling. For much too long I had worked in jobs where all I had ever done was chase the clock around. I was glad eventually to get out of the building for all of the reasons that I mentioned, but I was getting more and more excited at the prospect of doing some undercover work later on that evening.

I never went home after my minor shopping spree; I decided to drive straight to the casino. I had been feeling a bit tired and didn't really fancy the idea of motorway driving at night after a long day. I was just about sick and tired with my job, if you can call it that with the financial services boys. I had made some lame excuse not to go into work and my sales manager was getting more and more irate by the day. I don't know why as it wasn't costing them a bean, as I was self-employed. But I had been making excuse after excuse, car accident, stress, you name it. I knew that my days there were numbered and I was grateful for the income that I got from a small private poker game, which actually paid my meagre expenses for about six months. You see that's the thing with me, I never chase money when I have enough for what I need in the immediate future.

Or is that just an excuse to mask my idleness or lack of drive? If I wasn't chasing money then what was I doing with this blackjack caper? A psychologist would say that I crave recognition and attention, and I wouldn't argue. I wanted to achieve something substantial, perhaps something that few others had managed. In a sad kind of a way I wanted people to admire me and respect me, but with blackjack the whole idea is to prevent anyone from knowing that you have this expertise.

That was a part of the game that I hated, it seemed so unfair that I could never tell anyone about what we were doing. The sad fact was that I couldn't trust anyone to keep their mouths shut, even my friends. I was going to start the ball rolling by going to a casino about 40 miles away. I had never been to this club before and I thought that it would be a good idea if I were to go on my own. The drive took just over an hour, by the time that I had parked up, and it was early evening as I walked through the town centre.

I went past a row of shops and some street vagrant asked me if I had any money to spare. I knew that I had a few coins in my pocket. There have been stories in the local newspaper where I live saying that some of these "homeless" people have big flash cars parked around the corner, but I was an easy touch. I reached into my pocket and gave the guy a 50p piece, for which he looked very grateful. I have always felt that there is something fulfilling about helping other people; if only more of us felt that way.

The worst thing about winter in England is that it gets dark very early, usually around four o'clock. The nights always seemed terribly long at this time of year. It took me a while to find the casino as all of the roads in the city centre looked the same to me and I had no map to help me. I asked several people and it was just my rotten luck that most of them were foreigners and the ones who were English didn't have a clue.

Eventually I found it, or I should say stumbled on it. There it was tucked away almost hiding down some dark side road. My heartbeat seemed to quicken when I saw the entrance to the casino. Here I was and there was no going back now. I could feel myself getting more and more excited, like some little kid who couldn't wait to see what Santa Claus had brought him on Christmas Day morning.

I walked up the steps into the reception area to be greeted by a couple of smiling lovelies. This was a far cry from the last casino where I had worked, where we had door men for receptionists. Nice blokes they were, but far from being easy on the eye like these two beauties. I went through all the usual procedure for a punter who was visiting a casino for the first time in England.

Within a couple of minutes they were done with me, and off I went through the double doors into a short corridor that led to another set of double doors. The lighting was subtle, just like it was in every casino that I had ever worked in. I was making comparisons already with where I had previously worked. Stop it Carl, because you are not here for that.

Why do casinos always seem like nice places to work in when you are just visiting them? Although gaming is not well paid compared with other professions, there are much worse jobs out there. What I used to love about the job was the fact that you never had to get out of bed first thing in the morning. I hated the sound of an alarm clock. I like to have a drink and a snack and a couple of hours pull round time before leaving the house, but day jobs don't give you that privilege.

Through the second set of double doors I went and here I was in the gaming area. I looked around to get my bearings with the new surroundings. It wasn't a very big casino, about a dozen tables or so unless they had any private rooms anywhere else. I couldn't see their poker room from where I was, but I knew that they had one because I had already inquired over the phone.

It was early evening, about 7.30, and there was not an awful lot of action happening in the pit –usual for this time of day in my experience. I decided that it might be a good idea to go and get myself a drink from the bar and take a seat for a few minutes to observe a few things.

As I sat with my glass of beer I took in the ambience of the place. The bartender had told me that the card room was on an upper level. I had hoped to be able to signal Steve in from the card room, but that tactic was obviously not going to be possible now. There were only a couple of roulette tables going and a single blackjack table open.

I had planned on staying for a few hours so obviously I couldn't sit here all night on my own without it looking suspicious. I thought that I would give it about 15 minutes and then go over and play a bit of blackjack. Everyone seemed relaxed and friendly, which is really how it should be, but I have worked in some places where the atmosphere has been terrible.

I was watching a female dealer over on one of the roulette tables. At first glance she didn't seem too experienced. Her chip cutting was very slow and cumbersome and she had spilled a couple of payouts when trying to pass them out to the punter. Then she took four attempts to spin the ball...an obvious trainee! Funnily enough, trainee dealers were not precisely what I was looking for on blackjack. The best ones are those who think that they are great and try to deal as fast as they possibly can in order to prove it.

The worst kind are the slow, experienced types who really don't care about showing off and don't deal fast enough to make many mistakes. I wasn't going to get much of an impression at this time of the day and I knew that I would have to stay quite late and see as many dealers as I could, although it was obvious that they had just had a new batch of trainee dealers. If you see one trainee dealer then there are likely to be others, as there are numerous people on dealer training schools and not just one or two.

This might have been bad news because blackjack tends to be the game that trainees get placed on the most. Although if ever Steve was hitting the table then any trainee dealer would be rapidly replaced by a much more experienced dealer, or even an inspector, especially when he started playing maximums. I wasn't overly sure if I had come to the right casino, as anybody who was playing table maximums in a place as small as this was going to get the management really sweating.

What I didn't want to do if I could help it was to make casino managers nervous. This was why I felt that it was imperative that we spread the action as wide as possible. I didn't want a situation to develop where the casino was expecting to be hit the minute that they saw the big player walk through the door. This was precisely the reason why I wanted known big players, because these people would be tolerated for much longer than someone who wasn't known.

I had finished my drink by this time so it was time to amble over to the blackjack table. The dealer who had been on that table had been there for a while so I felt that they were due for a break. If I were to go over there and play now, then I could assess a couple of dealers in a very short space of time. I suppose that one of the advantages in hitting a smaller casino is that they tend to have fewer staff.

It would be perfectly possible to look at a dealer's weaknesses on blackjack and then not see them deal that game all week because of the number of staff that they had. We needed a casino that had numerous dealers who had weaknesses, not to mention dealers who had easily trackable shuffles. I didn't like the idea of John or Kevin attempting to track a shuffle that was too complicated as I was not overly confident about their ability.

I arrived at the blackjack table to see a small young kid called Ian dealing the game. I used to hate wearing name badges when I worked in the industry. Some arsehole who didn't even know you would insist on always calling you by your first name like you were best mates or something. It drove me crazy! I was surprised to see that the table had a £500 maximum – this place was not as small as I had thought at first.

A £500 maximum may not seem a lot to American readers, and maybe it isn't because that is under $1,000, but in England it is rare to see anything higher than that outside London. So this club was prepared for a bit of action after all. There were two other players at the table, both playing no more than a few pounds per box. I asked how the table had been running; this doesn't matter but it is an entirely normal thing to ask for an average player.

"Not too good," was the reply.

"Maybe opening another box will alter your luck," I commented.

The table minimum was £2 per box. I may have been here for a very serious reason, but I wasn't here to play serious blackjack. I only had about £200 on me so I didn't want to do anything stupid like run out of money. I asked the dealer for singles (pound chips) and passed him a £20 note. I was only going to be playing table minimums and could possibly ramp it up if I started winning.

The purpose of this trip was not to play blackjack but to scout the place and anything else would have been a distraction. No sooner had I bought in than the dealer exposed the cutting card to reveal the final hand. I was sitting in the centre of the table, because first and third bases were occupied, which was not ideal. This looked to be a very relaxed place; dealers would openly have conversations with inspectors and vice versa. I had worked in some places where the staff would be warned about this.

As the dealer took the cards out of the shoe I could see that this was a six-deck game, which was not good if you were a counter, but not a disaster for us. I carefully scrutinised the dealer's shuffle and there was nothing fancy or complex about it at all; even John and Kevin could track this without any difficulties, or at least I hoped that they could.

I casually started to engage the staff in simple conversation, which is never a bad idea. I asked them what their poker tournament nights were – Mondays, Wednesdays and Saturdays. I watched Ian complete the shuffle. I was certain that I could have seen certain cards if I wasn't so tall. A person who is six foot like me has to get too far down in his chair to see flashed cards, but someone smaller like Patty is already down there anyway, god bless her little soul.

I placed £2 on my box as the dealer prepared to deal the

opening hand of the shoe. Penetration was not great as he cut a good two decks from the back, but once again that would only affect traditional counters. There was no point in counting because the shuffle tracking software would find the high card clumps anyway, and even if I had more money on me then attracting attention would not have been the best thing to do at this stage.

Besides, I know that this sounds horrible but I really didn't like the idea of putting my money at risk, but putting somebody else's money at risk was fine. I just didn't have enough money behind me then to start risking everything that I had. I was confident that we would earn money but it was far from guaranteed;, besides, what guarantees does life come with? All that I had experienced over the past few years was heartache and bad luck, and this could easily turn out to just be another hard luck story or some guys with big, unworkable ideas.

Let's face it, the world is full of people who have ideas that have bummed or never even got off the ground. I would have been overjoyed with a few thousand profit at this stage. The dealer began the round and dealt me a stiff (slang for a hand between 12 and 16), it was 13 to be exact and the dealer had a 6, which is a great busting card. In a flash he pulls a 5 and a 9 to make 20, and my money is gone.

I put my money out straight away, even though I have lost. I give the dealer every opportunity to pay my losing box. This is a tactic that can make games with shuffle tracking machines profitable. When you play accurate basic then you are only labouring under a 0.5 per cent disadvantage and one single error per hour from a bad dealer can push your expectation into the positive. When a dealer makes an error and they realise it too late, most simply shrug it off. They think that the recipient is a degenerate, losing gambler, who will lose it back eventually anyway. The overwhelming majority of them are, but not this baby.

He does not make an error on this hand, but I will always give a dealer the opportunity to pay me twice or to pay me for a losing hand. Dealers have personal problems like everyone else and many a time their head will simply not be in the game.

Just then the lady on the first box decides to cash in. Here is my chance I thought. I look up to see three members of staff come out of a door to my left. That must be the staff room and these three must be coming back from a break. It looked if I would be getting a change of dealer. I could see the television in the bar area from first base so I make this my excuse for the reason for my seat change. I quickly place my £2 on the first box and get to see one final hand from Ian before he is taken off the table.

Ian seems quite slow and deliberate, and not the obvious type to make plenty of mistakes, but I don't let that get me down because there are plenty of other dealers in the gaming sea. I was trying to get an estimate of just how many mistakes we could take advantage of in an average evening, so I could calculate a better estimate of an hourly rate. Although even if I could pin this figure down to a precise number, calculating an exact hourly rate would still be an almost impossible task.

Ian's hand beats mine again and he is off with a smile to be replaced by an older girl called Leanne. She appears giggly and excitable, just the type of dealer to make an error or two. I had been in gaming for so long that it still felt very strange to be sitting on the other side actually doing the punting. I kept telling myself that I must not do any chip tricks. This would be a sure fire sign that someone could possibly be ex-gaming.

Although I have seen some punters do amazing things with chips, it does tend to indicate someone who is use to handling them an awful lot, which of course croupiers do. Whenever a dealer is on an empty table then there really isn't an awful lot else to do and it can become very boring, so you end up playing with chips to relieve the boredom and of course over the years this leads to dealers being able to do certain tricks.

Although I am not the most dexterous person in the world, I could ring alarm bells if I started doing the wrong things with the chips. I make a mental note to put the bet out normally and not to do anything with my chip stack, which is more difficult than it sounds because there is a tremendous urge to want to touch them and play with them. I remember having these same urges the first night that I met my partner, Angela, although that had nothing to do with chips.

I need to see if Leanne is exposing flashed cards so I subtly slip down in my chair a few inches. Leanne is a typical confident fast dealer; something tells me that she hasn't been dealing for all that long. She had been on three different tables in the short length of time that I had been here and she had not inspected any of them.

It is common in certain casinos for inspectors to deal games sometimes when there is either a big game going on or a shortage of dealers. It is also rare to see dealers who are still dealing after three years because 18 months' experience seems to be the minimum requirement for dealers to be promoted up, although I have known it happen both sooner and much later than this.

I was promoted after 21 months, which I think is about the norm. Leanne seemed a nice girl with lovely, long-flowing hair and a charming manner. After about six hands, I still hadn't spotted any flashed cards, but I was certain that they were there. She was applying too much pressure to the centre of the card and was almost pulling the card out of the shoe before the players were indicating for one, due to impatience.

I couldn't slide any further in my chair without it looking as if I was either drunk or asleep but I was certain that Patty could exploit this. Now if you are looking for a classic example of why a guy who is 30 years old is still struggling for money, then here it is. I have done an awful lot of stupid things in my life and I am prone to impulsive behaviour which has certainly not done me any favours, but what happened next really took the biscuit.

In her eagerness Leanne pulled a card to her hand, when she already had 17. Her error was a classic dealer's mistake: she started with an ace and pulled a 3, which gave her a soft total. But she pulled the cards so fast that she had miscounted her own hand. She had already reached 17 when she pulled another card and that card was an ace.

Now the rules in many casinos state that in this scenario the card is placed under the shoe to be the first card dealt on the next round. Same old story. In my eagerness to do something clever I reached into my pocket and took out the remainder of my money and tossed it to the dealer. She looked quite startled as I had only being playing £2 per box. She counted out the £180 and asked me what denomination chips I would like.

I asked for ponies (slang for £25 chips) and she passed me seven of them with a £5 chip on the top. I immediately put the lot on first box. What in god's name was I doing? I was supposed to be here on a scouting mission and not to draw attention to myself. I could easily have lost the bet even though my first card was going to be an ace. All I would then have had left were a few pound chips which could have gone in an instant and that would have meant no more blackjack because I had neglected to bring my plastic with me.

Leanne looked across nervously at the male inspector, a grey haired guy in his late 40s called Ron. He gave her a quick glance and then glanced at me with that "fucking smart arse" look on his face. Of course, I knew that they were both hoping that I would get shafted on the hand, but the dealer was going to have to best me with me having an ace start, and that was very difficult.

With luck they would see me as just some opportunistic prick who would eventually get his just desserts and get his ass kicked. Mathematically, the move was 100 per cent sound but betting almost everything I had irrespective of the 50 per cent edge or so that I had was not the smartest thing to do. If I were going to be frequenting this casino often then I wouldn't have done it. All the same, I should have left myself a bit more money to play and scout the club with.

Of course I could have stayed on the table even if I had no money, but then you look like some pathetic sad case who has done their money in and just can't face going home. I have seen thousands like that so I know how pathetic they look. Leanne and Ron said nothing but the rapport that we had been sharing suddenly disappeared. They no longer saw me as their "friend" but as some low life out to capitalise on an unfortunate error by a poor little defenceless female dealer.

My eyes widened and my pulse quickened as she dealt the cards. It was only £180 and it was not going to make or break me either way, but this was their mistake and I wanted to punish them for it. If there was any justice in this godforsaken world then my pay back was going to start right here and now, this minute. In an instant Leanne, not dealing quite as fast now, deals herself a 9 and plants a big fat juicy jack of clubs on top of my shiny red ace to give me a blackjack.

With the payment of three to two, I win £270 on the hand. I can almost see a big imaginary scoreboard lighting up: "CARL 270, GAMING INDUSTRY 0". The confidence that flowed through me when that bet went in was absolutely priceless. The look on Ron and Leanne's faces when I calmly put the chips into my pocket and placed a mere £2 on my box for my next hand was even more priceless.

I was now doing what I had been setting out to do, and that was to beat blackjack armed with a strategy based around shuffle tracking and exploiting dealers' errors. It was only the beginning of the war and many more battles had to be fought, but I was off to a flyer. To put the icing on the cake we had also agreed that any money that I won on the scouting missions was mine, and that went the same for losses as well.

Suddenly I felt ten feet tall and the casino staff, who had seemed like grim reapers when I walked through the door, suddenly looked like vulnerable targets ripe for attack. Confidence cannot make you a winner in blackjack but it sure can help when things start to turn bad for a while. It is great not just in blackjack but in any form of gambling to have known good times.

I have recently been through some pretty bad runs in my online poker career but my losses have never exceeded my wins, and long may that continue. But I wonder just how many good blackjack players and poker players out there have packed it in because they had an unbelievable run of bad luck right at the very beginning and had never had the chance to build up the confidence to plough through the bad times.

You see that's just the thing with many books, they quote the mathematics and the slide rule boys talk about this and that, but many of them don't really know what gambling for a living is like. At this particular point of my career neither did I, but at least I admitted it.

The atmosphere on the table changed in an instant. Leanne and Ron were laughing and joking no more and I got the distinct impression that I had just made a couple of enemies. I didn't care, though I was a bit concerned about my momentary lack of discipline, which could have wiped out all the money that I had on me at the time. I was hoping that what had just happened would remain on the table and that the pit boss or the management would not be informed. I suspected that they wouldn't say anything because after all it was their mistake, and it would reflect badly on them. They would prefer to keep it quiet. I had done the same thing numerous times myself.

Leanne was a very erratic shuffler and hopefully her shuffle wouldn't be the norm, but it seemed to me that she was on speed or something, because I had never seen anyone as hyperactive as her. Her shuffling might have been a problem for tracking but it was presenting many more opportunities because she was flashing cards to me several times throughout the shuffle. I was in the perfect spot to see them at third base, and she was not squaring the cards up when she placed one shuffled segment on top of the previous one. At the end of this particular shoe, I had the cutting card and she exposed enough of the back card to indicate that the card was a picture and it was a spade.

Now I knew full well that when you know that your opening card is going to be a 10 value card that this gives you an edge in the region of 13 per cent. Meaning that you will return £113 for every £100 wagered in the long term. Of course the long term in gambling can be very long and a lot longer than many people think, but with a 13 per cent edge behind you, it is nowhere as long as it is for a conventional counter, or shuffle tracker for that matter.

Now for the test, I knew that they were not going to let me cut just one card from the back, as most casinos insist that you cut at least half a deck. I had done tremendously well in practice doing this at home, but these were different cards and suddenly my confidence evaporated into thin air when it came to wagering money. Besides, I couldn't guarantee that this card would land on my box and it would look very odd if I suddenly placed a sizeable bet on someone else's box without doing so on my own.

I cut what I thought to be 26 cards from the back and if my estimate was correct then card number 26 would be that spade picture card. I watched as Leanne placed the shuffled cards back in the shoe and proceeded to deal. There were only 17 cards dealt out on the first round of play so my target card was going to arrive in the next round.

My mind was racing so much that I had not heard Leanne ask me if I wanted a card or not. I looked at my hand and I had twelve, a quick look at her card revealed that she had a 10. I took cards to leave my total on 19 and hardly noticed when she pulled an ace to her picture card to get a blackjack and wipe the table out on that hand.

Even if I was out with my estimation then this wouldn't mean that the tactic was useless, only that it required more work. My eyes were focused on the table like never before; there were three players on the table playing four boxes, so this meant that card number 26 would be the player on third bases second card. My eyes followed the action like a cat follows a mouse and there it was, *Bang!*, the queen of spades precisely where I thought it would be and to make it even better there were no other picture spades near it, so that had to be the card that I had seen. My heart was racing and I was imagining all kinds of things and most of them were pound notes.

I was so excited that I retired back to the bar for another drink although I would have to be very careful because I was driving back home on my own and didn't want to risk going over the limit. This was one of the most exciting things that I had ever done, demoting having sex for the very first time into a distant second and even beating the birth of my daughter, although that was more fear then excitement at the time.

Or maybe it just felt exciting because my life had been relatively dull for so long and suddenly I was James Bond, or at least it felt like it. That card being exactly where I thought it would be was fantastic and if this happened once then it was sure to happen again. In fact Patty would have observed more cards than I had if she had been sitting where I was.

What this meant was that I could even go it alone for a while if push ever came to shove, and Steve and the boys dispensed of my services after I had trained them. This had always been my greatest fear and all sorts of things were flying through my head as I sat there sipping my drink. I was wondering how much of a bankroll I would need with an edge of 13 per cent. Surely it couldn't be that much. I didn't know the answer but I knew that I could find out.

I began thinking about cover plays and camouflage tactics if I were ever to start playing on my own. This was far more exciting than card counting, which seemed very dull by comparison. I sat there and watched as I saw Ron being taken off for a break and being replaced by a female inspector. I carefully watched him approach the pit boss to fill him in on how the table was doing, which I knew was standard procedure. I was looking for any sign that he was informing the boss of what I had done, a shake or flick of a finger or a head, a subtle glance in my direction, but nothing happened.

I thought as much: no member of staff would admit a mistake to their seniors and especially one that cost them money. There and then I had an idea to increase the longevity of the team – to perform certain moves only when pit bosses and managers were not present. It was common to see a duty manager wandering around the pit in most casinos. This was a good sign in a way because at least it meant that they were not watching you on CCTV from some office somewhere.

The pit boss or manager rarely came to the table unless it was losing money. Most of the time they just happen to be passing or make polite conversation with a member of staff or a punter. The pit boss tends to come over every hour to do a check, which gets logged onto a pit sheet, and the information is then passed on to the duty manager in turn and even the general manager if they are present in the building.

Yeah, I thought, we will do this because what dealer or inspector is going to inform the pit boss by saying something like "Blackjack 1 has just dipped a grand because Leanne twice pulled a card when she shouldn't have and the guy on first base lumped on and I didn't stop her because I wasn't watching...sorry." It's just never going to happen. Punters get away with an awful lot when the managers are not around because many inspectors just let it go, especially those who haven't been inspecting all that long. They don't like the pit boss to get involved if they can help it because it suggests that there is something going off on the table that they cannot handle; they don't want to look or feel stupid and incompetent so they cover it up if they can. I have done it countless times and so has every single one of my workmates; you just switch off for a second and something happens and you just tell the dealer to pay it.

Let's face it, when it is not your money you really don't give a rat's arse. You might get the odd conscientious inspector or dealer, the type who kisses arse with the best of them or thinks that being a pit boss is a major step up in life. But apart from them, most staff are generally pissed off about something and this is why the staff turnover is so high in many clubs. It is precisely the reason why they get targeted for collusion, because the charlatans and the cheats know that most staff are not happy with their lot. But if you were a gaming manager and you asked a dealer or inspector if they had ever been approached out of work by a punter to cheat, then who on earth is going to say yes. For a start you are supposed to report such things, but it is rare that anyone does. Besides, it is only certain members of staff that get approached anyway.

So I sat there collecting my thoughts and being rather relieved that my little incident had not been reported. I decided to go back to the table because Leanne was due for a break. I knew this for certain because it was almost time for the night shift to begin. There had been very promising signs so far with numerous dealer errors and bad shuffles.

Back on the table, the third base was still vacant so I quickly took a seat there. I had already cashed in my chips and had to buy in with cash once again. I started where I had left off by betting only £2 per hand. After just a couple of hands, the staff room door opened and a large group of gaming staff came out. This was obviously the night shift and I would get the chance to observe another dealer.

The two dealers that I had seen so far had done nothing fancy with the shuffle but their pick sizes seemed erratic, which if it continued would present us with a bit of a problem. This was especially the case when I wouldn't be there in person to supervise what was going on. One little success on third base and I was starting to feel invincible; come on Carl get a grip of yourself.

Leanne seemed to have tightened up on her dealing after what had happened earlier, and she was still not making any more small talk with me. In fact she made this very obvious because she was happily chatting to the other two players. Suddenly I realised another reason why we would have to spread our play among as many casinos as possible: these dealers would have very long memories when it came to being taken advantage of. At least with counting and shuffle tracking the methods are subtle but this was just blatant opportunism and dealers wouldn't forget that in a hurry.

Leanne announced that this would be the "last hand before a new dealer". I looked at her replacement who was a tall, thin kid called Tony. I noticed straight away how big Tony's hands were. Handling cards didn't seem to come entirely naturally to him, but he was far from being a rookie. He wasn't the chirpy chatty type that Leanne had been, but he did seem to have some rapport with the new inspector. Football seemed to be the topic of the day with these two and once again we had a relaxed atmosphere as both men were oblivious of the move that I had performed a short while ago. As football is a passion of mine, I found it very easy to get involved with the conversation.

Tony was about six feet four or so and he had developed a stoop while dealing. I felt that this kind of posture would present possible opportunities for us because there was no way that he could have been comfortable at the table in that position, as I know from past experience.

The shoe ended so it was time to concentrate and get to work watching Tony shuffle the cards, though I had to carry on being involved in the conversation with these two about football. To have stopped talking now and started concentrating intently on what Tony was doing would have looked very strange. I realised that I could count cards and carry on a conversation with unbelievable ease, but it was a lot harder to watch someone shuffle and carry on a conversation at the same time. At least with counting you actually get moments of "down time", but I had to watch Tony's shuffle very closely and your eyes cannot be in two places at the same time.

I would probably have to tone it down a little bit with the chat otherwise I might just be wasting my time being here. Suddenly I noticed that Tony had done exactly the same thing as Leanne, he had exposed the back card while shuffling. Not only did I know that this card was a picture, I also knew precisely what card it was. No one in particular had the cutting card so I casually picked it up. Tony completed the shuffle and offered the deck for me to cut.

I cut what I believed to be 26 cards from the back. I knew that it had to be at least half a deck from the back because I had heard Leanne point this out to one of the other players earlier, who had tried to cut less. The card that I had seen was the jack of diamonds without any shadow of a doubt, but I still was not in an ideal situation to do anything about it. I watched as Tony dealt the cards one by one, but on this occasion it fell that the first card out of the shoe for a new round was going to be card number 26.

As Tony was paying the winning hands after his own hand had busted, I was quickly trying to determine what to do. Should I lump on with a 13 per cent edge? But that is hardly the same as it is for an ace...I bottled it and placed £20 on the box, which still looked very heavy as it was all in singles and ten times my usual bet. I knew that this would look odd. Gaming staff understand that counters increase their bet size and I would run the risk of correctly being black-balled, but for the wrong reason.

It wouldn't be as bad as this with the big players, which was precisely why spotters couldn't be the ones to bet big. In a flash, I stood up before Tony dealt the first card and claimed that I was getting tired and needed a drink and that I was going to "go out with a bang", which amused the pair of them.

"Let's see if I can deal you a blackjack," remarked Tony with a cheeky grin.

He started to deal and in a flash the jack of diamonds appeared on my box as my first card. Played two won two, I thought to myself, bang on the fucking button both times.

"That's half of it," I replied, but there was no happy ending with this hand, as my second card was an 8. Tony was also showing an 8 and I was expecting a stand-off until he pulled an ace to make 19.

"Sorry about that," said Tony.

I replied something like it was "only money" and that it wouldn't be a bad thing if I had less money to spend at the bar.

Sitting back at the bar to collect my thoughts, I did a quick check of how much I was up – exactly £264, as my basic strategy bets had also won a bit of money.

The best news was the sheer number of errors that I had noticed and I was beginning to think that shuffle tracking may not be needed, although I couldn't tell the others that. Shuffle tracking could only add to our profits if we did it correctly, which was a big "if" in my opinion, but some of these moves were simple money earners as far as I was concerned. I must confess to sitting there and wallowing for far too long in what I had achieved, but I had found out what I had come here to find out: that this was a very laid-back casino and the first few dealers that I had seen all had predictable shuffles and exploitable errors. This was not the type of club that would tolerate losing too much money, but no club would tolerate that. "Casino A" as it will now be known will definitely be a target for us in the not too distant future.

Several hours later, I decided to call it a night and head for home. I had run my winnings up to almost £400 and I was ecstatic. I walked out of the casino feeling ten feet tall but I was only too aware that this was only the opening battle and this was going to be a very long war, or at least I was hoping that it was. But what had happened tonight had given me ideas, a lot of ideas. So many ideas in fact that I didn't even fear coming up against a shuffling machine; after all, they are still operated by humans and, as I had observed tonight, these humans cannot be trusted to deal the game properly and professionally half the time.

The truth is that today's dealers don't seem to know what dealing professionally is and the casinos themselves are using very bad dealing procedures. I had looked at the games that were going on down in the pit both on roulette and blackjack, and I could have pulled the games to pieces because of how weak the dealers were. Even members of staff who dare to call themselves experienced are vulnerable simply because they have never been shown correct dealing procedure.

What casino staff fail to comprehend is that cheating methods are far more advanced these days and this calls for a change in how the dealers are dealing the games – this must start at the very beginning on the training schools in my opinion. There are far too may gaming staff out there who think that they are the dog's bollocks when it comes to dealing.

I have worked with people like this, people who think that they know it all but have only ever worked inside the same casino year after year. I mean, just what kind of experience is this? Have you got ten years of experience or tens years of experiencing the same things? There is a world of difference but I am certainly not complaining because as long as the casinos think that they are safe then they are vulnerable.

I knew that we couldn't hit any one club too hard because that club would certainly alert other clubs if they ever cottoned on to us. It wouldn't be as bad with recognised big players, but I hadn't spoken to Steve to check on what progress he had been making down this channel. I figured that it was best if I also pursued this avenue myself and didn't just sit around waiting for Steve to make something happen. I knew a couple of people who would be well up for this because they had approached me while I was still in gaming.

My mind was in a spin with all of the stuff that was flying around inside my head as I walked through reception on the way out. I stopped at the desk to get my jacket and I made some small talk with the staff while I was waiting.

"Are you working over Christmas?" I asked them.

"Yes unfortunately," said the taller and prettier one of the two.

I smiled in sympathy but I had been there many times. It was kind of ironic that I had hated working over Christmas for the exact same reasons as these people. Not spending enough time with the family at this time of year seriously annoys gaming staff. Now that I was no longer in gaming, my marriage had broken up and suddenly I have got all of the time in the world over the festive period. I put my jacket on and headed for the exit.

"Merry Christmas, Mr Sampson," said the girls almost in unison.

"Same to you."

Chapter 10

Onward Christian Soldiers

January 1999

I am always happy when Christmas is out of the way as it has too many bad memories. They seemed to get worse by the year and Christmas 1998 was especially bad. I lost my dear Mum and a close uncle within the space of five weeks in May and June 1999. If my dear Mum could have seen me now she would have been proud of me, I am certain. She wouldn't have understood much about what I was doing, but then again most people wouldn't. It's surprising as you go through life how certain dates and places seem to take on a new significance. There are not many worse things in life than losing someone who is very close to you to help you put things into perspective.

Nothing much had happened over the festive period and Steve and the boys had their own plans and schedules – we kind of unofficially decided to start proceedings in the new year. I had several conversations with Steve and informed him of my successes at Casino A; he was over the moon with excitement.

I was rather excited myself and hated the down time over Christmas because I wanted to be doing something productive. But I suppose the others had loved ones and kids, not to mention grandkids, so I couldn't really complain just because I was on my own. I got a severe case of itchy feet a couple of days after Christmas and decided to do some more scouting, but this time I headed south and encountered Casino B.

This was yet another club which I had not been to before and it was very similar to the first casino in many ways. There was a similar size pit area and I wouldn't have minded betting that the casino's turnover was in the same ballpark area as well. This club had four deck blackjack and slightly lower maximums on all games including roulette. Once again I witnessed numerous exploitable dealer errors and I left this casino breaking even, but certain in my own mind that we could do very well here.

However, Steve had informed me that John and Kevin had not been putting any practice in over the festive period with the shuffle tracking and the other stuff. Kevin's attitude angered me because if I had my way then he wouldn't have been in the team. He seemed to be too interested in drinking and womanising than putting in the work. People like him think that the world owes them a living and that money is just going to fall into their lap. Maybe it does for certain people, but just how many people does that apply to? Certainly no one whom I have ever met.

I told Steve what I felt about Kevin and made him promise that our conversation be kept confidential. He told me that Kevin was OK and would come good. I thought Kevin seemed to be a very dangerous team member to have, but it was Steve's money and he wanted him in, so what could I do?

I had arranged our first session back at Casino B with Steve and Patty. They had never gone there before, which was good, and in fact they had never gone to a casino as a couple before, as it turned out. I called Steve to arrange a short briefing session at his house just to get it absolutely clear what each of us were going to do. John and Kevin wouldn't be there, much to Kevin's annoyance, because he felt that things were starting without him and that things were going to be happening behind his back.

"Are you certain that you and Patty have never been to a casino together before, Steve, because I thought that I recalled you saying something the other month that you had?"

Steve looked puzzled: "Don't know where you have got that from Carl."

The point was that Patty was going as my partner because she was young enough to pull this off; we couldn't have Steve approaching the table and betting big when his partner was sitting at first base. There was a small re-buy poker tournament happening on this particular night and Steve would be playing. I wanted to get there nice and early so I could get Patty on first base.

We were all going together in Steve's car, but he would drop us off as we got to within about half a mile of the casino. I would never rule out the possibility of us being followed when we left, although I couldn't see this happening on our first visit, but it was something that might happen if we were suspected of playing together.

"So we are not going to be shuffle tracking tonight, Carl?" asked Steve.

"No, we'll just do the advantage plays and see what happens," I said.

To be honest, I didn't fancy the thought of being under too much pressure immediately and getting it wrong. I could feel the pressure building as we were driving down the motorway. This was a very serious test for me; for Patty it would be easy. She knew basic strategy now and all she had to do was concentrate on the cards without it looking too obvious.

The long stream of car headlights going in the opposite direction seemed hypnotic. In fact I have always hated motorway driving at night for this very reason, but fortunately Steve was the one who was doing the driving. Steve was very excited and never stopped talking, which in a way I was thankful for because neither Patty nor I was making any conversation.

Steve's constant talking was helping to ease my nerves and I couldn't help feeling guilty at my motives for not wanting to shuffle track. I should be taking this thing head on and be big enough to face the consequences if it went wrong. But a part of me wanted John and Kevin to get it wrong so that no blame could be attached to me. Cowardly! You bet it is and I bitterly regret now that I didn't play the Hollywood tough guy at the time.

This was the time to try shuffle tracking because if I failed then Kevin and John's chances would be diminished severely. I should have been the test pilot and not them, because it was I after all who had the most skill and practice. Or maybe I was in fact doing the right thing by not rushing anything? Yeah, that's right, Carl, make yourself feel better.

"What time does this tournament start," asked Steve.

"Nine," I replied. The plan was for Patty and I to walk in as a couple and for Steve to follow us about 30 minutes later, but for there to be no contact between us. I wanted Steve to be in the bar when we signalled because the bar was quite close to the black-jack tables and it wouldn't take him too long to get over to us.

We had discussed the issue of Patty going with me, which Steve felt may cause a problem if she was later to go with him or someone else. Patty continually coloured and bleached her hair, which changed her appearance dramatically. The key to this entire thing would be to spread our action as widely as possible so that no one club would be hit for too much money.

By the time that any discernable pattern emerged, if it ever did, we would hopefully have taken a large amount of money – at least that was the plan. If we could get off to a winning start tonight then that would do wonders for our confidence, not to mention Steve's. He still wanted to attack roulette and never stopped pestering me to go down this avenue. I felt that if we made a good start then that would go a long way towards shutting him up.

We had decided that Steve would drop us off at the edge of the town centre and we would walk the rest of the way. It really doesn't matter which town centre you walk around at night, they all seem depressing and intimidating after dark. I made small talk with Patty as we walked and I really couldn't help noticing how attractive she looked in her dress. She had a charming personality to go with it and I was certain that she would bewitch the male croupiers.

"What's your natural hair colour, Pat," I asked.

She laughed and said "Do I really colour it that often?" I had seen Patty several times now and she hardly ever seemed to have the same colour hair from one visit to the next. "It's actually brown but I don't like that colour."

I smiled and said "I think it looks nice."

Stop it, Carl. You're flirting with another bloke's bird here. This is supposed to be professional behaviour and my starting the whole evening off by leering after some woman was hardly professional. We reached the casino after about 15 minutes and I was much more nervous than when I had come on my own. I think it was because when Steve was signalled in, he wouldn't be messing around with the size of the bets and this would draw attention.

Steve would love this kind of attention because he was a natural extrovert, but I wasn't and neither was Patty. I hoped that I wouldn't start looking nervous, as I have a tendency to blush easily. I mean why should someone blush and look nervous when someone else is winning money, or at least that is how they would see it. I signed Patty in as my guest and within a minute we were walking through the lobby.

I thought that we had better not overdo it with the husband and wife thing, because Patty might come back here with Kevin or John and she could be recognised. I told her to head straight for the blackjack table and take first base, as we couldn't be certain that it was going to be free later on in the evening. Casinos usually get quite busy on the nights that they have poker tournaments and this would be no exception.

There were two tables open and Patty asked me which one she should go to. I looked at both of the dealers and didn't recognise either of them from the previous visit so I told her to take her pick. I didn't want us both to go directly across to blackjack so I went to the bar to get myself a drink. Steve was doing the driving so I thought I would indulge in a little drink, although one was enough as I needed to stay mentally sharp.

I had briefed Patty and she knew exactly what to do. I had instructed Steve to play very aggressively in the poker tournament because we couldn't afford to waste the entire evening with him getting to the final table and busting out just out of the money. This isn't the world series of poker: you had to get into the last four or five places to get any money. If Steve was knocked out shortly after the re-buys finished then that would suit me fine. It was only a very small re-buy tournament so getting knocked out, even if it was deliberate, would be no big deal and just another expense that could be tagged onto our cover.

I had been in the bar for about ten minutes when I saw that Patty was already getting chatted up, which was no real surprise. But I didn't want her to be distracted unnecessarily so I thought that it was time for me to get over there.

Mr Chat-up soon exited stage left when I arrived and it became obvious that we were a couple. Single women seem to stand out like a beacon in casinos simply because there are not that many of them. Casinos in England aren't places that single women frequent on their own. The ones that do tend to attract men like lights attract moths, the attractive ones that is.

I asked Patty how it had been going and she looked up and smiled and said that it had been going well. This signal told me that she meant that she was seeing cards and plenty of them.

Who on earth was going to perceive her as a threat? I certainly wouldn't have if I had been dealing. We had been here about 30 minutes and I took a subtle look around to see if I could see Steve anywhere.

I couldn't see him but we had agreed on being 30 minutes apart so he wasn't going to be far away. Patty gave me a look as if to say that she had not seen him either. I sat down on third base and bought in for £20 of singles. I had not even placed my first bet when I could hear Steve's booming laugh coming from across the pit. He was talking and laughing with someone about something. Steve was the type of person who could make friends at the drop of a hat.

Either that or this guy was someone whom he recognised. I thought that this was a good thing because if Steve was talking and joking with other people then it wouldn't look as if he had come with us. I knew that Steve had five grand on him in cash and we had another five grand hidden in the car. We had arranged to have a couple of betting opportunities before the poker tournament began if the chances arose.

Steve disappeared from view in the direction of the card room, presumably to buy in. I knew that you had to buy in for a certain time and Steve was getting pretty close to it. The one thing that didn't make me feel entirely comfortable was that my presence didn't look quite right if I wasn't playing poker. This was something that we couldn't afford to repeat too often in my opinion.

I looked across at Patty and the look that she gave me told me that she was having tremendous success at spotting flashed cards. The great thing about this tactic is that it is not cheating. If a house dealer is careless enough to expose cards then that is their problem. It is the same with poker: if a house dealer reveals a card accidentally and only one person spots it then that is not their fault.

I didn't know about Patty or Steve but I could feel my excitement level rising. The maximum on this table wasn't all that big, just £300, but that was certainly high enough to do some damage. The dealer was on a great run of cards and I lost my initial £20 in no time. I was covering all my basic strategy expenses myself, but I knew that I wasn't losing money in the long term.

It is pretty simple to extract money from a blackjack game even if you are not counting or tracking, and this even includes games with shuffling machines. I didn't want to risk the success of the team on a few cheap shots on my own behalf. I didn't want to draw attention to the table above and beyond what Steve would be bringing shortly.

What I liked about the layout of this particular casino was that Steve would be nearest to first base from both the bar area and the card room. It would have looked odd if he had by-passed six other boxes to stick a maximum bet down on first base if the table and the set up had been the other way round.

The dealer was a lady in her mid to late 40s who was probably an inspector because it was rare to see someone of her age who was still a dealer in England (although it is common to see this in Vegas). Her name was Catherine and she was dark and Spanish looking. She was very quiet and didn't go for conversing with punters, or least she wasn't conversing with us.

She busted from an ace, which was a novelty as she had been in a rich vein of form since I had arrived. Suddenly, without warning, Steve appeared from nowhere and placed a large bundle of notes on the table. Catherine counted it out to reveal £500 and she politely asked Steve what denomination chips he wanted. Steve calmly said that he wanted ponies (£25 chips) and the Catherine took a stack of ponies from the chip tray and cut and proved them to the inspector.

I looked at Patty who was acting superbly. She must have

signalled Steve in without me realising it. Before we go any further, I am not going to be revealing our signalling methods…sorry folks but that is just too sensitive I'm afraid. Steve quietly placed £250 on Patty's box and the dealer and inspector visibly became more attentive.

My heart was pounding and I had to try really hard not to look too closely at the first card that was dealt. Why is it in these circumstances that you feel that everyone in the entire room is on to you and knows precisely what you are doing? Probably for the same reasons that people who have nothing to hide and have done nothing wrong get paranoid when they are in close proximity to police officers.

The first card out of the shoe was the jack of hearts, so a big well done to Patty. The dealer planted an ace on my box but I didn't give a shit, to be honest, and I wished that they would have planted that ace onto Steve's jack. The dealer gave herself a 3; that was good but in an instant she drew a card to Patty's box. In consternation I saw that the card was a 4. Patty looked at Steve to ask him what to do, as I had instructed her to. When a minimum bettor has just had someone put down a near maximum bet into their box, then the natural thing to do is to ask the bigger player what they would like to do. Most players don't want the responsibility of possibly losing someone else a large chunk of money and Patty was playing it to perfection. Steve motioned for no card and the dealer made her way around the table, finally ending at me.

I had to place my hands under the table out of sight, because I could feel them shaking, not from fear but from the adrenalin rush. I had 19 and took no card and the dealer made 18 – our money was gone in an instant. Played one lost one: Steve cracked a joke and walked back up to the bar area. There was still 30 minutes before the poker tournament began so there was still time for a couple of other opportunities.

I didn't like this situation. It sounded great in theory but it didn't feel right. I couldn't shake off the feeling that we would get caught playing this way. Patty and I were not locals and yet we were in a casino 60 miles away and we were not playing poker. Many of the things that I said that we shouldn't be doing and would never do...we were doing them.

I wasn't supposed to be here and team members were supposed to be playing poker. It was hardly a great start. We seemed to be getting carried away with it all and to say that I was far from happy would be putting it mildly. A few minutes later, with the same dealer, Patty signalled Steve in again. I cringed as I saw him approach the table on what would be the first hand of the shoe again.

Steve placed another £250 on the box. This felt all wrong. It just seemed too obvious – or was I being paranoid? Then I couldn't believe my eyes when the dealer pulled an 8 to Patty's box as her first card. What the fuck is going on, does she need glasses or what? My heart sank when the dealer pulled a 5 for their card and then another 8 to Patty's box, to make 16 and a splitting situation.

Steve knew that Patty had cocked up but he also knew that he had to split the 8s. He reached into his inside pocket and took out another wedge of money to hand to the dealer. I could see the inspector trying to get the attention of the pit boss, which was normal in a situation like this. The dealer counted out another £500, making Steve in for £1,000 now.

The dealer parted the pair of 8s to make two separate hands. To my horror they pulled another 8 and a 3 onto the 8s, giving Steve another split and a double situation. Steve didn't have enough in chips on the table to cover the double and the split, so he had to buy in for a further £500.

I was trying to look nonchalant as the dealer put the £25 chips on the table. God only knows what Patty must be feeling at this minute. The entire thing was getting off to the worst start possible and if this hand went pear-shaped then the entire venture would be seriously undermined. This was a good situation mathematically, but we possibly stood to be down £1,500 if it all went wrong.

I knew full well that Steve was not the type of person to sit back and lose his entire bankroll so, in effect, we didn't have the bankroll that we thought that we had. This meant that it was crucial to get off to the best start possible just to calm our initial nerves and fear. The dealer split the second pair of 8s and Steve ended up with a 10 on one and an ace on the other for 18 and 19. Decent hands, but you could hardly take it to the bank and we were being made to sweat.

To make matters worse, the dealer gave Steve a 4 on the other 8 to make 15. It seemed to take forever to get to me as everything seemed to happen in slow motion. My mind was in a whirl as I was thinking about Steve up in the card room for the next two hours dwelling on losing fifteen hundred quid in the blink of an eye and then starting to doubt the entire thing.

Jesus, we have barely started and already we were fucking up. I knew that I hadn't made the error but I was the one who had placed Patty into that situation and so had effectively given her the job. This was all my idea and my creation; these people were here in this casino on this night doing exactly what I had told them to do and when. So I was to blame and no one else.

I know that whatever cards I take, it makes no difference in the long run about what happens but countless players criticise people who play on third base if the dealer happens to make a total. All I could see was the dealer pulling a 6 and then a picture to their 5 to make 21 and wipe us all out and maybe even our chances as well.

As it turned out, I had a total that dictated that I took no cards, but I still put on the act of asking Steve what I should do.

"Just play your own money, pal, and don't worry about mine," was Steve's reply. I took no cards and watched as the dealer starting to pull to her own box. Catherine seemed to take forever to pull the cards as she straightened her hair first and then pulled the cards more slowly than she had previously.

The bitch was deliberately making Steve sweat, but if only she knew the truth, that two other people around this table had a very keen vested interest as well. The first card was a picture to give her 15, oh come, please…please. My silent prayers seemed deafening to me and I was certain that other people could here what I was thinking.

Catherine pulled the next card and as she started to flip it, my heart sank as a red 6 gave her 21. I started to look away when I heard "Get in there you fucking beauty."

Startled, I looked up to see Catherine grabbing hands full of ponies to pay Steve out. I did a double take on Catherine's cards; it wasn't a red 6 but a red 7 and a beautiful 7 of hearts at that.

I stared in disbelief as Catherine emptied her float and had to start paying Steve out in £5 chips. The manager turned up at the table at that moment with a refill for the float. He had the false happy look that I had seen many thousands of times. I did a quick calculation in my head and that hand put us ahead by £750, although very fortuitously it has to be said. Steve exchanged his piles of £5 chips for ponies and walked off to the cash desk.

Patty looked nervous and agitated, and also a trifle embarrassed. I tried to make light of it by saying how difficult it was to be responsible for all that money by being on third base. Several people nodded in recognition, but Patty didn't seem to hear me. She appeared to have drifted off into a trance and seemed very troubled by what had just happened.

She wasn't the only one. Steve was not stupid and if he felt that the operation was not working then he would quickly pull the plug. He didn't seem the type to be overly patient if things went wrong. In fact the entire operation could have ended there and then if that hand had have turned sour. But luckily for us it didn't and we were ahead.

We never got the chance to signal Steve in again because the public address system announced that the poker tournament was starting. I was glad about this because it gave Patty the opportunity to calm down. By this stage there was only a single seat between us and I took the opportunity to place my hand on her arm, purely as a calming gesture and to reassure her that everything was indeed all right, that these things happen.

But come on, Carl. Surely you don't seriously expect to walk into any casino and walk out with tons of money as easy as that? By the end of the night, we had signalled Steve in on three more picture card situations and I was tracking the shuffle very well, although I still wasn't signalling Steve in for that. I hated feeling pressured with my decisions and it was a far cry from doing it in practice sessions. Playing with someone else's bankroll was easier on your own pocket, but it was still incredibly nerve wracking.

Or at least it should be if you give a damn. We ended the night £1,250 ahead, and for any casino bosses who happen to be reading this, don't bother checking back through your records because I have altered the totals.

As we left the casino walking arm in arm for show, I finally had the chance to ask Patty what had gone wrong with the first hand.

"Carl I swear to god, I honestly don't know. I saw a picture I'm sure of it but it just didn't come."

"I really would forget about it, Pat, if I were you," I said.

"Do you think that they cheated us, Carl?"

"No, definitely not. That kind of stuff doesn't happen over here it's purely legit," I replied

"Does seem odd though or maybe I need glasses," she said.

I laughed and said "There's more chance of you needing glasses, Pat, than them cheating."

Steve's car was parked exactly in the spot where we had agreed to meet and Patty thought that we really ought to stop walking arm in arm at this stage although, to be honest, my mind was so active that I had never realised that we were in fact still walking arm in arm. As we approached the car Steve started the engine and we both climbed in, with Patty getting in the front and me in the back. I wasn't the least bit surprised by the first thing that came out of Steve's mouth.

"So what happened back there darling?"

That was a relief, at least he wasn't being abusive to her, but I could hardly vouch for what would happen when they got home.

"I've just been talking about it with Carl and I can't explain it. I am certain that the card was a picture."

"Can you explain it, Carl? Did they suspect what was going on and pull one on us do you think?"

"That's what Patty said, but casinos over here don't go in for that sort of stuff, Steve," I replied.

"You sure about that?"

"100 per cent, well 99.9 per cent actually," I said.

We all laughed along and I was massively relieved to have got out of there with a nice win under our belts. But all didn't seem well with Steve's manner; he just didn't seem happy to me. The rest of the journey went by in relative silence as our fatigue set in. Steve eventually dropped me off at about 3am – I was supposed to be up at 7.30am for work.

I was almost on the verge of leaving the job, and was getting fed up with the pestering phone calls from my manager wanting to know when I was going back. Still, at least we had won and I had earned myself some money in the process, well in theory anyway.

CHAPTER 11

D-DAY – IN MORE WAYS THAN ONE

February 1999

This was shaping up to be one hell of a day. My sales manager at work was at the end of his tether with me and had called a crisis meeting at 9.30am. I knew that it was going to be volatile because I had not been into work since before Christmas. To be honest, I should have left a good couple of months ago and spared everyone the grief and anguish, but it had just dragged on and on and only I was to blame for that.

I was very unhappy at the way that I was being asked to work and I could spend the entire book talking about the reasons why I was so pissed off with this firm. Take it easy, folks, because I will refrain from doing so. I was right, though, because the meeting was intense: my sales manager knew that I had been bull shitting for the better part of two months about why I had been off work.

I was lying through my teeth and he knew; he also knew that I knew that he knew, if you get my drift. I won't bore you with the details but, needless to say, I left the office out or work, although I resigned voluntarily before I was pushed.

Driving home, I was contemplating what I could possibly do for a living. Blackjack couldn't be expected to supply me with a living despite the positive start. I may be somewhat of a dreamer at times but I am not stupid enough to put all my eggs into that very dodgy basket. I wasn't worried as I knew that I had options and could phone up at least half a dozen people for a job, although most of the jobs – if not all of them – were not ones that I wanted to do.

I could also go back into gaming but that would be the final straw. I would hate to have to go back with my tail between my legs cap in hand. I didn't have an awful lot of time to dwell on it because tonight was the night that John and Kevin were entering into the fray, again in casino B. This was to be our last outing at this club for at least a month as I didn't want to hurt them too much or be noticed too much, either. It was crucial that we spread our action as thinly as possible and two consecutive visits to the same club was stretching it in my opinion.

We had one final session at Steve's place where I put John and Kevin through their paces. I was surprised just how far they had come in such a short space of time. I was having problems trying to get the team to do exactly what I wanted and at times it felt as if Steve was running the show, which probably pissed me off more than it really should have, because, after all, it was his money.

As soon as I got home, I grabbed a bite to eat and made sure that there was plenty of charge on my mobile phone. I had to do everything from the confines of my bedroom as my two flat mates were not at work until nine in the evening and it was likely that we would be in conversation before then. I couldn't allow Paul or Robert to know what I was up to; they already knew too much about my knowledge of blackjack as it is.

I had the laptop fired up by 7pm as I knew that the four of them were scheduled to get there about this time. I hated not being able to see what was going on: what if they couldn't get a signal? What if they cracked under pressure? What if we lost heavily? What if they were making too many mistakes? All of these thoughts were flying around inside my head as I sat there in my bedroom staring at the mobile every few seconds, wanting it to ring but apprehensive about it ringing all the same.

Time started to drag so I started to read a book. I couldn't go far because once my phone rang they would need an answer about the shuffle very quickly.

At exactly ten minutes to nine the phone rang. It was Kevin. My heart rate must have increased rapidly; in fact it would have been interesting to measure it at that particular moment in time.

"Hi Carl, it's Kevin."

"Thank god for that, I was starting to get worried, thought that you couldn't get a signal or something."

"Relax. Steve's in the poker tournament now but I need a fix on this shuffle and I was just trying the phones."

"Have you placed any action yet?" I asked.

"Not had the chance yet," said Kevin

"Where are you?" I replied.

Kevin chuckled and said "In the toilet, obviously, but it's not easy to talk as people keep coming in."

Shit, I had not thought of that. "Give me the details then, Kevin, quick."

"He's doing exactly the same shuffle as what you've got programmed but he's picking up about a full deck whenever he shuffles."

"A full deck! Has he got shovels for hands or what? Is John still at the table saving your place?"

"Yeah, don't worry, it's all in hand."

"Get back to you in two minutes Kevin…and don't forget to turn your ringer off."

I hung up and rapidly set to work. This dealer, whoever they were just highlighted the potential problems with this technique. We were wasting time making these phone calls when they really should have been on the table and by the time that we had an angle on certain dealers they were going to be taken off for a break.

But if we were going to shuffle track at all, then I really couldn't see a way around this. I just wished that I could get myself in there and help them although who was I to talk? I had my chance to show what I could do and I bottled it.

I dragged up their house shuffle on the laptop and quickly input full deck grab sizes and started the calculation process. About a second later, I had the answer on where the high segments were going, based on the strategy that we had agreed on. I had just told John and Kevin to keep it simple and to merely track the cut-offs, which is a basic shuffle-tracking strategy and not too complex.

It wouldn't give us the edge that advantage play would give us but it would mean that Steve wouldn't always be coming to the table on the first box all of the time, either, which I thought would create an identifiable pattern. I rapidly called Kevin back but I couldn't get through.

"Jesus Christ come on." I couldn't raise my voice as there were other people in the flat with me at the time, but I felt like shouting. I tried again; I was waiting for what seemed like ages before Kevin's mobile started to ring.

"Yes, get in there."

Within a second Kevin answered, "Hi Carl, make it quick because I am losing the signal."

"First half of the shoe and don't ma..." The phone went dead. I immediately tried to call Kevin back but couldn't get through. This wasn't working; I tried again only to find that he had turned his phone off. He must be back in the pit now. I was trying to calculate how long Steve would be in the tournament for. He was no Doyle Brunson but you didn't have to be to win or do well in one of these small re-buy tournaments.

Back when I was in gaming, there had been cases where players who I had shown how to play the week before had got to the final table the following week. That is in no way a reflection of my poker ability, just how much luck there are in these things. Paul and Robert had left the flat by this stage to go to work. I used to hate being in the flat on my own but now I was loving it. Isn't it funny how times can change very quickly – but this hadn't just happened, I had made it happen and that seemed immensely satisfying.

Just over an hour later I got a second phone call; this time it was John.

"Hi Carl!"

"How's it going John? Is Steve back yet?"

"Just seen him walk past me. Kevin's up five hundred."

"What do you mean Kevin's up five hundred?" I asked.

"He's played a couple of hands that were close to the maximum on his own," replied John.

"What, you mean without Steve being there?"

"Yep," said John in a rather disgusted tone of voice. "I didn't even realise that he had that much money on him," he continued.

"What the hell is he doing? There will be enough attention when Steve starts betting without giving them two players on the same fucking table to concentrate on," I replied.

"You try telling him because he sure as hell won't listen to me," said John. "Anyway I need a fix on this dealer, same shuffle as before but she's picking quarter to half-deck picks."

"Leave her alone, John, and tell Kevin to do the same if you get the chance. This sounds too risky to me." I said.

"OK, talk to you shortly Carl."

John hung up. What the hell was happening to us? We were a disorganised and undisciplined rabble, we wouldn't last a week playing full time like this even if we did manage to spread our play about. I sat there in my room contemplating no longer having a job and my dream of being a professional gambler, for want of a better phrase, going up in smoke on the very same day.

I was wondering if I really should be taking a more active role by being there myself. Was I guilty of taking the easy way out? One thing for sure, people in any field don't succeed by taking the safe route or by crapping themselves. When the going got tough, where the hell was Carl? I'll tell you where I was, hiding behind John and Kevin, that's where.

If we failed then it was their fault, because they didn't carry out my instructions. Yeah, that was right, I could say that I suppose. For god's sake, Carl, stop it. Think positive. If this was going to get anywhere then I needed to demonstrate to all of them that I could do it and not just in theory, either. How could I hope to convince them that tracking worked if they had never seen me operating under real conditions?

I had never operated under real conditions. If I couldn't do it then what chance did they have? If Kevin and John failed then I would forever be asking the question, "Could we have succeeded if I had been there?" I couldn't risk both of them doing anything more complicated than tracking the cut-offs, and this was hurting our earning rate as well.

I couldn't decide on the right course of action and my head was in a spin. If I got this right then I wouldn't need to find a job, or at least not straight away. But I knew that I shouldn't make a knee jerk reaction just because Kevin the maverick had done his own thing. Maybe I should go off and play more on my own. I had already had some success but I knew that this would harm the team as I would be playing and getting noticed in casinos where the team would probably end up.

I received another call about 40 minutes later; once again it was John.

"Just give me some good news," I said.

"Same dealer as before; he's back on the table again but I forgot what you said," said John.

I ignored John's question, "What's happening with Kevin?"

John laughed and said "I think Steve gave him the evil eye. There's going to be trouble after we get out of here between those two."

"Great," I said, sarcastically. "Any more action going down?"

"We got an ace situation about half an hour ago. Steve hit them for the maximum and got a blackjack."

"Fantastic. No one's listening to you are they?" I was frantically talking and typing at the same time. "Bottom half again, John," I said without waiting for the answer to my previous question, "but make sure the count is sufficiently positive."

"Yeah yeah, I know," and with that he hung up again.

I clapped out loud and shouted, "Go on Stevie Boy." A blackjack on a maximum bet was a real boost in the arm for us, although I would only be truly satisfied when I received my money.

I received three more phone calls that evening and everything seemed to be going well, despite the earlier display from Kevin. The upshot of it all was that we finished the evening ahead by almost £4,000 but the team was far from being professional. Kevin was proving to be everything that I new he was, erratic and a real pain in the arse. On top of that I couldn't trust him, he was unhappy about the percentage that I was receiving and he was sure to bring this up with Steve and John behind my back.

We had scheduled a debrief at Steve's place as usual for the following day when John told me that Kevin and Steve did indeed have serious words in the car going home that night. From what John told me, Kevin backed down in the argument when Steve threatened to throw him off the team. Kevin couldn't go it alone and he knew it. He had minimal success as a counter but this didn't stop him from talking the talk.

We have all met people like Kevin: loud, brash and fucking experts on everything. Even when you told him something that you were certain he knew nothing about, he would still say "Yeah I know". You felt like smacking him at times.

The debrief at Steve's went smoothly despite my fears of a possible confrontation with Kevin because I too struggle at times to keep my mouth shut. I think that all the arguments and shouting had blown themselves out in Steve's car. If there were any problems and we certainly had a few, it made sense to sort them out because although I didn't like Kevin, I didn't want any ex-team members floating around at this early stage. Ex-team members get jealous and jealous people have careless and vindictive mouths, and we couldn't really afford that. We had scheduled another session in three days time with just me, Steve and Patty again, but in another casino.

Kevin was busy, which was hardly surprising, and John had to go to a funeral. It seemed to me that Kevin was more concerned with spending time at the pub than coming with us and this wasn't the first time that he had skipped a meeting. We needed to get something sorted out with the percentage payments, because it was becoming apparent that various people were putting in various amounts of time, and it would be unfair to pay everyone the same rate. What pissed me off was that Kevin was the one who had been spouting off that I should get a lesser percentage because I wasn't physically present and the rest of them were.

I needed to have a word with Steve before our next session because there were numerous things that I wanted to discuss with him, least of all what was happening with the other proposed big players. We arranged to talk the following evening and made the arrangement out of earshot of both John and

Kevin. They probably would have suspected some kind of conspiracy if they heard us arranging this, although it was perfectly innocent. We stood on Steve's front door for about 15 minutes telling jokes and stories, but I knew that all was far from well. We were due to split the money up the following week and there were going to be changes. Should be fun I thought.

CHAPTER 12

RUSSIAN ROULETTE: IT'S THE ONLY GAME IN TOWN

I hate cooking. All that preparation and you eat the thing in a few minutes. It is different when you have a family because you have to make the effort, but cooking always seemed like a boring chore to me. So here I was again sitting down to sandwiches and crisps with a cup of coffee. I really should be thinking about doing something with my diet because I was not eating very healthily and hadn't been for some time. In fact the only time I ever ate properly was when I was with a woman.

The phone rang at 7.30pm. I had seen to it that we had a cordless phone because I couldn't have the kind of conversations that we had been having with the team when I was standing in the hallway. It was Steve, calling at exactly the time we had prearranged – he was always punctual.

"Hi Carl. How's tricks?"

"Oh, not bad, Steve. Yourself?"

"Pretty good as it happens."

"So what happened the other night between you and Kevin?" I couldn't wait to ask this although John had already filled me in. I wanted to hear Steve's version.

"Oh, he thinks that he's in charge at times. I just had to drag him back into line that was all."

"I couldn't believe it when John told me what he had done while you were playing poker. What was he thinking?"

"God knows, but that's Kevin for you," replied Steve. He chuckled and said "But he won't be doing it again."

Steve was a very pleasant guy, great to be with, but you always got the impression that you should never cross him or you would seriously regret it. What bugged me about the guy was that after all this time, I still wasn't sure what he did for a living.

"Listen, Steve, we need to talk about a few things."

"Yeah I know we do," replied Steve.

"First, we are due to split the money up next week and I don't think that it's fair when different people are putting in different amounts of time. Kevin has been missing meetings and I know that John is not happy about it," I said.

"Well, he hasn't missed any casino sessions yet, so I think that it's best to just monitor the situation for a while and see what happens," said Steve.

"Another thing I'm not happy about is what we are doing or rather not doing inside the casino. We are not employing enough cover and you haven't made any cover plays on roulette yet."

"I know, Carl, sorry about that I just kind of got carried away."

"We can't afford to let this happen too often, Steve, and it's like this thing with Kevin, we are losing discipline at times. You know that we stand to win a lot of money with this but we have got to get it right."

"Yeah I know, we ought to arrange another meeting." Steve laughed, "We seem to have more meetings than sessions."

"There's nothing wrong with that because preparation is everything."

"Can you make it on Sunday round at my place, usual time?"

"You know me, Steve, I can make any night."

"Getting back to roulette for a minute, I was talking to a guy I know who would be interested in meeting you."

"What for?"

"He wants to pick your brains about roulette."

"Who is he? What does he do?"

"Let's just say that he's a businessman and he wants to put a team together to hit roulette."

"Hit roulette in what way?"

"I don't fucking know, do I, that's what he's hoping you are going to tell him. I just told him that you are ex-gaming and that you know stuff and he asked me to ask you if I can give him your phone number so that he can ring you."

"Not sure that I like the idea of some guy having my phone number. He might be a psycho or dodgy or something."

"Dodgy, tell me someone who isn't dodgy. Listen, Carl, these guys are serious and they won't be messing around. I can vouch for these people and if you do right by them they will pay you well and this could be a very good earner for you. Don't bullshit me now, Carl. Can you beat roulette? Yes or no?"

"Yes."

"What by having someone on the inside?"

"Don't need to do that, Steve."

"What then? You said that past posting was too obvious."

"There is more than one way to skin a cat."

Steve wouldn't let up firing questions at me: "Do you have a system or something?"

I laughed out loud, "No, there are no systems that beat roulette, not systems in the traditional sense."

"Anyway, his name is Tony and he comes from Reading. Am I OK to give him your number?"

"Yeah of course you are but I would much rather have his number."

"Don't worry, Carl, he's all right and he's not going to come looking you up if things don't work out, either. You know my feelings on this, we should have been hitting roulette instead of messing around with blackjack," said Steve.

"It's really not that simple, Steve, but I will give this guy my attention and I will listen to what he has to say. But I'm not getting involved in anything dodgy and if he doesn't smell right then I am not taking it any further."

"Fair enough," said Steve

"Anyway, lets get back to blackjack," I said. "Have you had any joy with recruiting any big players since we last talked?"

"There's a guy I know from London who's well up for it and he's got the money as well, he's already a known player. The casinos love him down there, he must be donating over fifty grand a year to them at least. His name is Richard and he works in IT, or some shit to do with computers anyway. Have you had any luck recruiting anybody?"

"Not yet, no. I had a couple of leads but they didn't go anywhere. I hate it when I get a knock back because I am paranoid that they are going to grass us up out of spite," I said.

"Yeah that always crosses my mind. We have to be doubly sure who we approach," replied Steve. "Anyway Richard wants to come up to have a chat with us one day next week if that is fine by you."

"I must be Mr Popular or something, everyone seems to want to talk to me."

"Probably because you are such a handsome bastard, Carl."

I laughed and said "I wish."

It was vital that we managed to recruit known big players or our lifespan playing blackjack was not going to be a long one. In fact I would go as far as to say that we probably wouldn't last until the summer if we were playing three or four times a week.

"I want to come with you on the next trip Steve," I said.

"By all means but I thought that you said it wasn't a good idea."

"I am not overly sure that it is but I think that I need to show Kevin and John how to track under real conditions. If they never see me perform then how can they have the confidence in the technique? Besides I don't feel comfortable giving them strategies that are too complex because I don't think that they are up to it yet," I replied.

"They both know their stuff about blackjack you know," answered Steve.

"They know *some* stuff, Steve, but nowhere near enough and they were never all that good at counting to begin with. Kevin just bullshits a lot and John seems economical with the truth, to say the least."

"What do you plan to do?"

"Like I said, I want to demonstrate to them both and to you as well that we can really do this thing, because unless we use the tracking and card steering methods properly then our earning rate is not going to be that high, especially not when we are dividing it among five people."

"This is why we need to be attacking roulette before we get busted," replied Steve.

He just couldn't understand that blackjack was my dream, this was what I wanted. I didn't just want to beat the casinos, I wanted to do it on blackjack. I had put in an unbelievable amount of work and practice over the years. Admittedly, I found the game very interesting and this made the practice very enjoyable for me, but it was work all the same.

I wanted to test my strategies and not only that. I wanted to try out my evasion techniques more than anything else. This roulette thing with the guy from Reading was interesting but a distraction, but if it was going to be an earner then I could hardly afford to turn down the opportunity. I could never envisage playing blackjack more than three days a week anyway, because of the problems of getting all of the team members free on the same day.

This was another reason in favour of me being there personally because I always made sure that I was available. Kevin and John, and especially Kevin, were enamoured with the prospect of winning money but were not too fond of working for it. After the conversation with Steve was over, I tried to relax and unwind for the rest of the evening but it was difficult with all of this stuff flying around inside my head.

Those sandwiches still left me feeling hungry, so the only thing to do in this situation was to make more sandwiches. I was about halfway through buttering the bread when the telephone rang. It was almost ten o'clock by this time. I wasn't used to anyone calling as late as this and I was hoping that no one was in any kind of trouble.

I answered the call to hear a strange sounding voice asking "Is that Carl?"

It was Tony from Reading. Jesus this guy doesn't waste any time I thought. I had only put the phone down talking to Steve about an hour ago. That meant that Steve had called Tony up almost instantly and gave him my number. Talk about being strong armed into something, these guys weren't giving me any piece.

I talked to Tony for about an hour and he came across as a really pleasant guy. I won't go into too much detail regarding the content of that discussion because it would be straying too far from the subject of this book, but he was putting a team together and wanted to know if I was prepared to come on board as a consultant.

We talked about a few things and he asked my opinion on loads of stuff; I could tell from some of the things that he said that he was ex-gaming. He knew a bit too much about the inner workings of a casino for my liking, and the thought of potentially being set up crossed my mind. As it turned out, Tony had been involved with a team of "top hatters" (past posting) down south but one of them had been a bit too careless with his mouth and had told someone who knew a croupier in the local casino.

The next time that they went in, the casino staff were ready and prepared for the move. The team never even got as far as cash desk because they were never paid out to begin with. Why is it that people think that past posting is really smart? Although if Tony was in fact ex-gaming, I was wondering how he came to know Steve. In fact that should come as no surprise now, from all of the bits and pieces that I had picked up over the past few weeks: Steve was one seriously dodgy individual.

But, like I said before, that didn't alter the fact that Tony seemed a genuinely nice guy to be around. I couldn't make my mind up whether getting involved with a separate team would be an advantage or a hindrance. If things started going badly for us and Steve found out that Tony's venture was doing well then I felt it likely that he would dump the blackjack.

What was I worried about, though, was that I hadn't put any money at risk yet and was unlikely to, so I was basically on a shot to nothing again. So what if they rumble us after a few weeks, what the hell I told myself. Stop being so bloody negative all the time, Carl. Be a bit more positive and you might just earn a few quid out of this thing – even if it was just enough so that I didn't have to worry about money for a while or getting a job for that matter.

Go down to Reading if necessary and meet Tony, talk to Richard when he comes up from London and stop worrying about being caught. But, like my dear old mum used to say, "Once a worrier always a worrier."

Tony had asked me the same thing as Steve had earlier: whether we needed someone on the inside and if so how could we do it. I told him exactly what I told Steve, that it was not necessary but it could be arranged if need be and I knew just the way to go about it. I even knew several croupiers who were approachable and who were slightly dodgy to say the least. I knew punters who were crooked and I also knew punters who knew punters. Yes, I have to admit that over the nine years or so that I had been in gaming, I had built a large portfolio of undesirables just waiting to be used.

But back to the blackjack: my conversation with Steve had ironed out a few things. I was happy in my own mind now with what everyone expected not just from themselves but from each other as well.

We had yet another briefing session at Steve's house. I pointed out what I wanted from the others and what we had been failing to do as a team so far. Kevin was strangely quiet and I got the feeling that Steve had really put him in his place the other night. Although you had to be careful with Kevin because he had the kind of personality that could erupt, especially if he had been drinking.

He was very opinionated but then again I cannot overly criticise that because so am I. But I didn't want Kevin to throw a tantrum and jack the whole thing in – he was capable of that in my opinion. We agreed that I would accompany Steve and Patty on the next session while John and Kevin put in some more practice.

Both of them hated the fact that some relatively young kid was telling them that they needed to know a damn sight more than what they already did and that they were not strong enough at their current level to win a meaningful amount of money. They never said anything but I could see what they were thinking in their eyes and the tone of their voices. But to be honest I wasn't really interested in whether or not I hurt their feelings as long as the team earned money. I was hoping that we would get to a stage where they would thank me for it in the end.

Everything seemed to be gaining momentum, what with Tony wanting to speak to me and Richard arriving from London in the next few days. Next week was certainly going to be a big week.

CHAPTER 13

THAT WAS THE WEEK THAT WAS

Now that I wasn't working, I seemed to have loads of spare time. Paul and Robert my two flat mates kept asking me what I was going to do for a living and they seemed terribly confused by the fact that I appeared to be showing no intention of looking for a job. It was getting to the stage where answering questions on this topic was becoming awkward.

My earnings from blackjack were slowing starting to kick in and what with the money that I was getting from playing in a pretty weak local poker game, I was doing all right for the time being. On top of that, my dear old mum and dad were for ever giving me money, a habit that they had never really got out of since I was a teenager, despite the fact that I was now approaching 31 years of age. But I was their only son and they were delighted when my mum found out that she was pregnant because, at 42 years of age, she thought that her chance had gone to have kids.

But the rest as they say is history and along came little Carl, one midnight in April 1968. I was born at the bewitching hour, so was it any surprise that I ended up working in a night job? I had always been a night-time person, even as a child. I always hated getting out of bed at the crack of dawn and I usually came alive around dusk. I am sure that if I were ever to meet Count Dracula then I would have got on well with the guy because we would have had an awful lot in common, though all that blood-sucking stuff seems a bit excessive to me and that might have posed a problem to a potential friendship.

So here I am in 1999, the night creature from hell back to haunt the gaming industry for all the hurt and wrong doings of the past, minus the fangs of course. I had managed to squeeze in a scouting session at another casino to the south of where I live and I had taken them for a couple of hundred without much fuss during the evening – this had been another confidence booster.

This used to be more than a week's wage for me not so long ago and now I was picking it up in a few hours. I have to point out that this was not my hourly expectation and that I could easily have walked out of that casino losing money, so I hadn't got to the stage yet where I could actually call it earnings as such.

The meeting with Richard went very well. He wasn't what I expected him to be at all. He was tall, charming and very well spoken, with a slight cockney twang from having lived in London for a few years, although he originally came from Cambridge. Richard knew the casinos in London well and he earned very good money working in the City. I got the impression that he was bored with his work and craved some other kind of stimulation.

Richard was single, as we all were apart from Steve, and he was a frequent visitor to the casinos in the south and a known big hitter by all accounts. He seemed to frequent these places for two reasons: boredom and having too much money for his own personal use. He drove a flash TVR, which was another indication or his apparent affluence.

We sat and chatted for a couple of hours before Richard went and met some friends that he knew in the area. We told him about our set up although I refrained from telling him about Tony and the other stuff that I had not even told Steve yet. Richard would be up and running with us inside a couple of weeks, which was fantastic news, although Kevin said that he wouldn't play too far away from home because of other commitments – no great surprise there.

This was precisely what we needed as team, a known big player who was already tagged as a "mug" by the casinos, and I mean this as no disrespect to Richard. Not only would we now be using a known big big player but I also knew full well that the maximums on blackjack increased the further south you went.

We had been handicapped so far as we had not been to a casino yet that had a maximum above £500. Although it has to be said, that was no bad thing after our less than perfect start. I had swapped phone numbers with Richard because there were still things that needed to be sorted out before we could proceed with a live session.

The kind of maximums that were on offer in the south would make the travelling well worth it and we could even go down for a couple of days or so and have a real good go at it. According to Richard, he was known all over the place and was a member of numerous casinos down there. He also knew numerous other punters and a couple of them were even willing to sign us in as guests.

We had arranged the same payment structure as we had with Steve, as Richard was also prepared to be the major backer in very much the same way that Steve was. This would mean that I could be playing or earning from blackjack at times when we couldn't play with Steve. His other business interests (I was still trying to find out what they were) frequently got in the way. Steve was fully prepared to let someone whom he could trust be the big player with his money in his absence, but we had not yet managed to find anyone.

Another great advantage of playing down in London and other areas in the south would be that there was less chance of me being recognised, although it was still a risk even down there. It would probably be John and I who went down, and possibly Patty if Steve gave her permission to go. Kevin wouldn't go and Steve would basically be a passenger and a liability because we didn't need an extra big player. I could have had him on first base but he wouldn't have been as effective as Patty. I would try to talk him into letting Patty go. Mind you, for all I knew, he might have been glad to see the back of her because I kind of got the impression that they had been having problems.

That was none of my business, but I did find Patty very attractive in a sort of older woman kind of a way, and that could have been a potential problem under certain circumstances. However, going down to London was not very high on my list of things to think about at this particular moment, nor was the quality of Steve and Patty's relationship.

What was on my mind was the up and coming session where I would be shuffle tracking live for the very first time. With someone else's money sitting just over my shoulder, about to be lumped on based on my visual estimation of the shuffle – this was definitely making me uneasy to say the least. I would have the laptop fully charged back at Steve's car, but it was a fair walk to the nearest parking spot and that would be a problem.

It was likely that I would have to operate on my own without the software to assist me and this was hardly helping to calm my nerves. I had really played the part of the salesman and talked the talk during that first meeting at Steve's with Kevin and John. I remember driving home that night feeling immensely pleased with my performance, but I had also placed a tremendous amount of pressure on myself.

I had been fine all week but on the day of the session I could feel my stomach tightening. I knew that this was likely to get worse and not better as the session got nearer. I didn't feel like eating at all, but I knew that I really ought to have something before I set off. I was very pleased that things were finally starting to happen but it felt slightly unnerving as well in a strange kind of way.

I was mixing with people who I wouldn't normally mix with and some of these people had powerful contacts. Steve's other activities, whatever they were, had an ominous feel about them. He never mentioned them – and just who was this Tony from Reading? He was all nice on the telephone, but then again he would be. There was a chance that I could be getting myself into a situation that I couldn't handle and I could easily find myself out of my depth. Not to mention that we would be seriously pissing off people from the gaming industry and there were powerful people at the top of that particular tree. We weren't taking the money from some duty manager or general manager. Casino owners are very rich and influential people who don't like it when things don't go their way. But wait a minute, Carl. Isn't that what I am supposed to be doing it for? Of course it is. Well, that and the cash.

I went through a few last minute strategies in my room before I set off for Steve's house. Not because I needed to at this late stage, more to calm my nerves than anything else. I arrived at Steve's place at around 6.30pm; Steve and Patty were already in the hallway with the front door open waiting for me.

"Early as usual, Carl. Are you ready to kick some arse tonight?" asked Steve with a smile.

"Hope so," I replied.

Steve's high expectations only served to heap more pressure onto me and I had to keep reminding myself that it wasn't my money that was at risk. Even if everything went horribly wrong then I wasn't going to lose everything that I had because I could easily pull the plug on my own participation any time that I wanted. I had totally shelved the idea of not paying up my share of the losses if we lost; the more that I learnt about Steve indicated to me that I wouldn't be wise in crossing the man.

Besides, there is always something honourable and gentlemanly in settling one's own debts. We made small talk for a couple of minutes before we set off. Even Steve was not his usual jovial self tonight. Either he and Patty had been arguing again or he had grasped the seriousness and importance of the session – and I don't think that my apparently nervous state did an awful lot to calm theirs nerves, either.

Steve and Patty would be going to this casino for the very first time and we were lucky enough to have someone who Steve knew to sign us in as guests. I had asked Steve if this guy had asked him why he wanted him to do this when Steve could have signed us in himself. He told me that he had just smiled and shrugged his shoulders as if to say "I don't want to know."

"Can we trust this guy to keep his mouth shut Steve?" I asked as we sped down the motorway.

"Don't worry, Carl, the man is spot on."

I had always known that to operate effectively we would have to bring more people in at some stage and this was just an occupational hazard as far as I could see. I thought that I had loads of contacts but Steve's network of people put my list to shame. He was always on his mobile talking to someone or other, doing some kind of a deal.

This casino had a card room but there was no poker tournament happening tonight. However, Steve's Chinese friends were due to play a cash game of some sort or other that wasn't poker, but it was a big hit with the Orientals. We would try and make that our cover as well, as the odd jaunt before roulette. I had instructed Patty to play the first base role again, which she had done beautifully so far.

"What's this place like Carl, can they stand a bit of action?" inquired Steve.

"It looks that way, but they also seem to know what time of day it is as well, so we are going to have to be a bit careful here," I replied.

"Are they a bit shrewd?" asked Patty.

"Hard to tell, but a couple of things that I saw and heard last time indicated that a few of the staff know a little more than the average dealer. We'll be all right though, Pat, don't worry."

I sensed her anticipation and slight fear; Patty didn't have the same cavalier approach of Steve and Kevin. She was a lot like me in many ways and if things had have been different then we could have made a good couple.

I directed Steve to our designated drop-off point from where Patty and I would walk the rest of the way and meet a guy called Alex just around the corner from the main door. As we approached the casino I could make out the shadow of a person standing in the doorway of some Chinese takeaway which was closed for the evening, just around the corner form the main casino entrance.

"I think that looks like our man, Pat," I said.

"Isn't this exiting? It's like something that you see in the movies," replied Patty.

I barely answered her. My stomach was starting to churn at the thought of what lay ahead and the sight of someone who might be Alex didn't do anything to help my anxiety. I desperately hoped that my actions and demeanour wouldn't give us away. All of the preaching that I had done to the others about not letting our cover be blown and to act the part and all the rest of it – suddenly all my confidence had evaporated into thin air.

I sure as hell didn't feel like an expert on blackjack who was about to give it to the casinos in a big way. The only result that I could see at this moment was being handed my arse on a plate.

This wouldn't be anything like what we had done as a team in earlier sessions or anything that I had done before. This was difficult stuff that I was undertaking here, and not some simple flashed-card strategy or exploiting dealer errors.

These were tricky strategies to execute and I didn't have the back up of the software to help me. Not in a realistic way, anyway, as the car was parked too far away for it to be feasible. I was untried in combat with this stuff. Sure I knew all of the theory, but knowing all of this stuff on paper isn't going to cut any ice. I kept thinking about Steve's reaction if I lost his money and that was hardly professional. But at this moment in time I was to professionalism what Adolf Hitler had been to world peace. Even if I was highly successful with the tracking strategies, we couldn't secure more than a few per cent edge at best, and that was nowhere near big enough to ensure a win over the session, which was basically what Steve was expecting, although he hadn't said as much.

Once again, I was contemplating dumping the tracking strategies in favour of the advantage play techniques. I couldn't make up my mind if we would be better off bringing Steve in a lot less but with a much greater advantage each time, or to really go for it with the tracking.

All kinds of thoughts were entering my head. What if we lost money and Steve lost confidence? Tony and Richard seemed to be good friends and he was certain to tell them about our failure and this was bound to affect their confidence in me. Come on Carl, you selfish bastard, it's not right to think like that. If you refuse to do the tracking strategies then aren't you guilty of putting your own self interests first? – Or am I deluding myself into thinking that I was concerned about Steve's money? Concerned about mine more like.

Everything seemed to be gathering pace and once again I didn't feel in control of the situation. I had the feeling of being swept along, not having time to think. Then I remembered how I was supposed to have thought and planned all this stuff, so what the hell was I doing? The fact was that dealing with reality was proving to be a damn site more difficult than planning the theory and putting in the practice. Isn't it always?

"Hi, I'm Alex. You must be Patty."

We introduced ourselves briefly, but didn't shake hands as we were unsure whether anyone was watching and we were only a few paces from the main casino door. Before I knew it, we were in the reception area and Alex was signing us in as guests. Patty looked cool and composed, as did Alex. But why shouldn't he? He didn't even know what was going on.

Within a couple of minutes we were inside the gaming area. I had told Patty to head straight to a vacant first base seat if there was one available and to occupy it for the night. I noticed that there was a different pit boss from the one who had been here the night that I had scouted the place. I was glad about this because I had caught the other pit boss making furtive glances at me; this had made me uneasy as I hadn't given them any reason to watch me. However, it was still relatively early so it was still possible that the guy could be on the night shift and was on his way to work even at this moment.

There was a vacant first base seat and Patty headed for it without it looking too obvious. I headed for the bar to get a drink to calm my nerves, which is something that I rarely do. Before I knew it I had ordered a double brandy – as rare for me as seeing rocking horse manure. I was almost teetotal and didn't drink much. In fact I didn't even know how much the drink would cost.

Looking back I suppose what was making me nervous was probably a combination of a couple of things: the thought of potential huge financial success (possible but unlikely) and worrying about the consequences of being detected, including what methods they might employ if we were. Come on Carl, for heaven's sake. This is England and they don't bump people off for winning a few quid – after all we were not cheating.

I was telling myself all sorts of stuff to ease my state but I was hoping that I would quickly settle once we began at the table. I casually walked across to join Patty; she had managed to secure first base, which was a great bonus for us. It was still relatively early but there was already a large Chinese contingent inside the building. I was told that they played all kinds of weird and wacky card games here and for sizeable sums of money, although the biggest game of the lot was Mah Jong. I bought into the game for £40 and looked up to see Alex peering across from the restaurant, looking attentive. He seemed to be very interested in what we were up to but there was certainly going to be nothing for him to see, not until Steve arrived, anyway.

I knew from my initial visit that the dealers were very shoddy here and this seemed especially so later on the evening. I got the impression that they were short staffed, which meant that a fair number of the staff were working double shifts. A 14-hour stint doing something that requires as much concentration as dealing roulette and blackjack takes its toll eventually, and that tends to kick in about midnight in my experience.

Staff who work double shifts tend to get an hour off between 9 and 10pm and they come back relatively refreshed both mentally and physically. But this tends to have worn off by midnight and they are not as mentally sharp by that stage. If you said this to any dealer they would probably disagree, but then again how many drivers think that their reactions are still the same after a few drinks?

Good dealers turn into mediocre dealers and mediocre ones turn into money earners. Of course, a dealer does not have to be tired to be weak. Many of them simply have a weakness in their technique, which can be exploited irrespective of whatever time of day it happens to be. The first six hands that I played at table minimum were all winning hands. I hoped that this was going to be a good omen for tonight.

Just then I caught a glimpse of Steve walking through the door and my heart beat quickened slightly: it was time to get to work. I was still waiting for this dealer to get to the end of the shoe so I could see his shuffle, but I was not going to be waiting long as he withdrew the cutting card to indicate the final hand of the shoe. He tossed the cutting card to no one in particular and I grabbed it instantly. I could see that Patty was doing her stuff but she was making it look a little obvious, must try and get word to her about that somehow.

By this time Steve had gone over and started chatting to Alex. There was no scheduled poker tournament tonight so Steve could be a lot more flexible about when he could come to the table to play. This dealer was exposing cards all over the place; I tried in vain to get an opportunity during the shuffle but couldn't manage it this time. He was exposing cards but not the ones that we could take advantage of.

The dealer completed the shuffle and I cut the pack. There would be plenty of opportunities to come tonight, I was sure. Now that I was actually seated at the table and was playing, my nerves had settled considerably. I still had that feeling in my stomach that we all get whenever we are nervous or apprehensive about something, but I felt in control for the first time tonight. I set about counting the decks that came out or I should say half decks because I always count half decks for shuffle tracking purposes.

I use chips to help me remember the different counts per half deck but any number of disguises or techniques would suffice. This was a six-deck game so I had to keep track of numerous different counts. Luckily, this dealer was shuffling to exactly the same pattern as the shuffle that I had stored in the laptop, but when I glanced quickly across to the other table I saw a young woman dealer who was doing something totally different. This is always the problem, of course, because many dealers have worked for other companies and move around a fair bit, and they take their differing dealing techniques with them. But anyway, I would worry about that later and I could always pop out to the car if I was in trouble.

You may be forgiven for thinking that I had made up my mind and decided to go with the tracking strategies after all. Don't bet on it. I was still all at sea about my best course of action. If I could be certain of success with the tracking strategies then the mathematically sound thing to do would have been to use them. But I couldn't guarantee success in the heat of battle and I also couldn't guarantee Steve's reaction to losing.

If we had a couple of losing sessions, Steve would pull the plug, I was certain of that. In fact it was a distinct possibility that Patty would be winning more money than I did during certain periods, if we were to cop for a dealer who was exposing cards to her on first base. If I started to lose and Patty was winning, I didn't think that Steve would have been able to have got his head around the situation. He still didn't understand the mathematics of what we were doing and why we actually needed a bankroll.

I had to make a decision and fast, balanced on my own interests (selfish I know) and trying to do the right thing. I finally decided that I would shuffle track and bring Steve in for a couple of situations and see how it went. If we lost those hands and went behind, I would stop bringing him in except for situations where I knew his money was going on a box with a 10 or an ace in it.

I can almost hear the mathematicians sharpening their knives, queuing up to tell me that I was wrong, and I couldn't argue with them, but it is surprising what pressure mixed in with a large dose of self-interest does to a person. All of the preparation in the world couldn't have prepared me for this; it went beyond just simple facts and figures.

In fact I didn't even know if I was cut out for this kind of thing at all, even with somebody else's money. My heart was beating so fast at times; I could feel it in my throat. This was supposed to be fun as well as an attempt to earn money. It felt more like a trip into hell from where I was sitting; in fact I am sure that professional gamblers have more health problems and a shorter expected lifespan than average. It always sounds great and exciting, especially when all you have ever done is read about it but reality is like a sheer rock face…cold and hard!

Before I knew it Steve was at the table playing £300 on first box, I was so engrossed with the tracking issues that I hadn't noticed Patty signal him in. It was strange, but the time between Steve arriving at the table and the first card appearing on first base seemed to take forever.

I really must try not to focus too hard on that first card. Why is it that every time that you are doing something that you shouldn't you think that everyone around you has turned into mystics and is reading your mind and is aware of everything that you are up to? The king of hearts hit first base like a sledge-hammer and I felt a little easier, but Patty's terrible error from a previous session hadn't helped matters.

My £2 on third base became irrelevant but I was struggling to concentrate on keeping the count while focusing on Steve's money at the same time. Hopefully the magnitude of what we were doing would wear off and Steve's betting would become almost a non-event to me. The dealer pulled another 10 to first base giving Patty 20, and the dealer's card was a 9. That hand would take some beating; the count was sufficiently positive for me to have strong hopes that he would pull a 10 himself to his own box and get us off to a winning start.

It wasn't a 10, but it was good for us all the same, as the dealer pulled an 8 to make 17 and a hand that they must stand on. Steve took his money and moved away from the table, but he wasn't going to be away for very long because if this dealer shuffled like he had been, then the count indicated that two high card segments were going to be married together.

Two more hands were dealt out before the cutting card was exposed. The first half of the deck was where the high card segment was going to be but it wasn't going to be more than about a 2 per cent edge at best. I signalled for Steve to approach the table slowly (we had separate signals for approaching the table, playing and moving away again). Steve was busy talking to Alex again but he wasn't moving.

I repeated the motion. Steve turned around and looked directly at me, but then continued laughing and joking with Alex. The dealer was placing the cards in the shoe and was about to deal. I removed my bet from my box and walked across to roulette to place a bet on even money. I knew that this tactic would stall the blackjack dealer because he would notice that I didn't have a bet down. I placed the bet on high numbers and gave Steve a knowing glance at the same time.

Strangely enough it was Alex who brought Steve's attention to what I was trying to do, although I didn't know how he could have figured that out. Steve must have told him. That guy really needs to learn to keep his mouth shut. I walked back to the table after a polite verbal reminder from the dealer that I had not placed my bet. Steve came across too, and placed the maximum on first box, totally contradicting what I had told him to do.

It was one thing placing a maximum bet when you knew that your first card was going to be a picture and having a 13 per cent edge, quite another to place a maximum bet with a puny 2 per cent edge. Of course, counters down the years would have given anything for a 2 per cent edge but these were different times. If Steve persevered with placing maximum bets in marginal situations then the first negative swing that we encountered would probably end our operation and the swing wouldn't even have to be all that negative.

Fortunately, we won the hand but I wasn't comfortable with the situation. I considered signalling Steve away from the table despite the fact that we could have extracted another four or five hands of this. I decided to let it ride and see what the next hand did, but once again Steve placed the maximum. The dealer and inspector visibly tightened up, which I expected. I could see the pit desk from where I was sitting and we were definitely getting attention now.

Once again we won the hand, although very fortuitously it had to be said. As long as we were winning I would let the situation ride and then try and get word to Steve when he was playing poker, or whatever wacky game they played in the card room. The next two hands were both stand-offs (a push) and the high card segment was over. I signalled Steve away from the table and he made his way to the cash desk to exchange his chips for cash. I knew that we had just had a close shave but thankfully it had gone well, at least that would do an awful lot for Steve's confidence as well.

I looked across to see a couple of guys in their 40s huddled in conversation. They were obviously gaming managers and it wasn't too difficult to work out what the topic was. I thought that it might be a good idea to give them some respite. Winning money too quickly and in large amounts would only serve to unnerve them and we couldn't afford for that to happen. If it did then word would spread on the gaming grapevine like wildfire and our days would be numbered. Drifting from company to company was no defence as I was aware that rival companies shared information.

In an ideal world I would have wanted Steve to go back to

any casino where we had won money and be seen to not play at all on at least one occasion, in an attempt to diffuse the situation, but sadly he didn't have time to do that. Also I would have liked Steve to be coming in on situations where we knew that his first card was an ace, but Patty couldn't tell the aces from the 4s, which is always a problem.

Over the next four hours, both Patty and I signalled Steve in on a variety of situations with mixed results. I had not been able to get word to Steve about over-betting, but I had not been signalling him in with tracking strategies anyway. We had a dealer for a full hour and a half who was very difficult to track and this gave me the opportunity to take a back seat for a while.

It was about 1am and things had gone badly over the past 30 minutes or so with four maximum bets all biting the dust. We had an absolute arsehole of a punter playing between me and Patty. He had tried to flirt with her several times when he knew full well that she was with me. This idiot was messing with the wrong guy, as the ability to turn the other cheek and ignore things is not very high on my list of strong points.

I had played a couple of hands on third base which had led to the dealer beating us all, much to the annoyance of Mr Ass. Every time that this happened I could feel his gaze burning into the side of my face. It was something that I had witnessed thousands of times from the other side of the table but now it was eventually happening to me.

Once again the dealer made a total that beat the table and this led him to say, "Sorry about that ladies and gents, I think that my luck's in tonight."

To which Mr Ass replied abruptly, "It helps when everyone can play."

That was it, the count had gone from my head. This asshole, who had only been here for about two shoes, had pushed me too far.

I leaned across, put my face about six inches from his and said, "Do you have a fucking problem buddy, because if you don't then I will be happy to give you one."

He was visibly startled and proceeded to try to explain that he had never directed any of his comments my way.

I was barely listening, but simply said "Just play your money and let me play mine."

Well, it certainly did the trick because at the end of the shoe he got up and left the table, once again uttering another apology, to which I just gave a silent, angry look in reply.

I was still annoyed and wound up. I never used to get agitated as easily as this in the past, but life had dealt me a bum hand and I was a different person now from what I used to be. My ex-wife always says that she doesn't know me any more. I had the cutting card in my possession and rapidly jabbed it into the pack, so hard in fact that it actually damaged a card by splitting it. I apologised profusely and claimed that I was still wound up by Mr Ass.

"Don't let him get to you," said the female inspector, in sympathy with my situation.

I smiled in acknowledgment but I then realised that the card that I had damaged accidentally was the ace of clubs. Suddenly I realised that this was a situation that I could possibly exploit. It would be interesting to see if there would be any discernable difference between the edges of the new card with the older used ones. These cards were about four hours old and had not been replaced, which was normal for blackjack.

Cards on Caribbean stud poker were changed every hour but nobody ever considers that it can be just as important to change them on blackjack as well. The game was held up for a while until the pit boss brought the replacement card. As it was inserted into the pack, I couldn't believe it when the edge was in fact slightly brighter than the other cards. It wasn't much but there was a distinct difference in shade.

This was a very exciting time because if we could get Steve betting with ace situations then we could really make hay while it lasted. There was only one other player seated apart from Patty and me, and he didn't seem to mind who cut. The dealer came to the end of the shoe and tossed the cutting card to Patty. I badly needed to get my hands on that card because Patty didn't know what I knew.

"The last time that you cut, sweetheart, we ended up losing," I remarked to her.

The fact was that she had never cut at all, but the current dealer and inspector didn't know that. Patty slid the card over and then it suddenly hit me: Steve wasn't here. I had become so engrossed in the situation at the table that I hadn't even noticed that Steve was in the card room. Alex was still playing on one of the roulette tables at the other side of the pit and I could get word to Steve through him.

It would seem very strange if I were to go into the card room, come back with Steve, and then he were to bet heavily on the same table that I was on. I knew that Alex must have some idea of what we were up to because of what had happened earlier. I slowly walked across to place an even chance bet on Alex's table. The dealer was busy chatting with the inspector and I had my opportunity. As I leaned across the table I softly whispered to Alex "Get Steve."

To his credit Alex grasped the significance immediately and went to the card room at the end of that spin. Steve arrived too late for us to take advantage of the situation on that hand, but the funny thing was that Patty signalled him in anyway on the second hand of the shoe. What was even funnier was that Steve ended up with an ace being dealt onto his 10 to give him a blackjack.

That was pretty ironic and amusing, because if I had been at the table he stood an excellent chance of hitting the same hand on the previous round, but the cards would have been the other way round with the ace coming first and the picture card second, although they wouldn't have been the same cards. I knew and had heard stories of some players deliberately damaging the cutting card in an attempt to damage a card whenever they cut the pack.

Obviously when you do this you cannot be certain that the card that gets damaged will be an ace or a 10. But five in every 13 cards dealt out on average will be an ace or a 10 and that is around 38 per cent. Doing this intentionally had in fact crossed my mind from time to time; I would be lying if I said otherwise.

But this was definitely cheating and the casinos would take a strong negative view if we did it – and there was no telling just what kind of action they would take if we took them for enough. This was another reason to spread our action as thinly as possible; it wasn't just for reasons of cover. It would have been very bad business to hurt any one casino too much financially; these places were not like the super casinos over in Las Vegas that wouldn't baulk at the thought of losing ten grand.

Of course, neither would most of the clubs in London but we were not going to be playing in the capital all of the time. We were ahead by about £3,000 by this stage, but in all of these sessions Steve had not done a single cover play on roulette as I had instructed him to. I didn't want to look at Steve in any way that could be identified as suspicious by the gaming staff, and I knew that the only way to get a message across to him was either by telling Alex, who was a known face here by the way, or doing the damn thing myself and hoping that he took the hint.

After a couple of even chance bets on roulette, I think that Steve finally got the message and placed one of his own...hallelujah. Steve placed £200 on red and my ears suddenly became the size of elephants as I was trying to listen to the roulette dealer behind me without turning round. I was keeping track of every bet that Steve made and what success he had been having. Not that I thought that he would rob the team, but I was just covering myself.

I heard the dealer announce "two…black…even" and knew that Steve's bet was a downer. I mentally subtracted a couple of hundred from what he was ahead by, and carried on with proceedings. After about five more minutes we once again came to the end of the shoe; time for me to get the cutting card again. I had been harping on about what a lucky cutter I had been so the only other player at the table was only too happy to let me take it.

The new ace was still only about 20 minutes old and was still ever so slightly visible. Never having done this kind of thing before with this brand of card, I had no idea how long the whiter sided ace would last. It could easily just disappear into the other cards after a couple of hours and then the opportunity would be lost, well for this evening anyway.

If Steve knew about the ploy of deliberately damaging the cutting card then I knew that he would be well up for this move. Cheating never stopped him before so it wasn't likely to stop him now. The dealer completed the shuffle and handed me the deck to cut. I carefully inserted the cutting card in front of the ace and the dealer as per usual placed the cut segment to the back – our golden card should now be the first card out of the shoe.

I had already signalled Steve in and he was ready, placing close to the maximum on first base. I smiled and said to Patty, "Looks like you are under pressure again, sweetheart."

She grinned and so did the dealer and inspector, who were relishing having a bit of action for the first time tonight. Sure enough, the ace of clubs hit first base and now my eyes focused on what the dealer's card was.

A 6, perfect. Now just put a picture card onto that ace. The dealer pulled a 4 to Steve's ace, which was a shame, and Patty asked Steve what he would like to do as part of the act. Steve motioned for a card, which was a 9, giving him a total of 14. No more cards for Steve but it was time to squirm on this one. It got to me and I did what I always do in this situation and just played the hands normally. I am not a mind reader and I do not have X-ray vision; if my play ended up costing us then so be it.

I had 15 and took no card. The dealer in a flash dealt two consecutive 7s to make 20 and our glorious situation bit the dust. Don't feel too sorry for us, though, because we managed to pull this situation on three other occasions, on which two were blackjacks. We had to call time on this tactic when I signalled Steve into a situation for what I believed was the ace of clubs…it wasn't! It was in fact a 9 and we also lost the hand.

What I had feared might happen had in fact happened: the new card was wearing in and the whiter edge wasn't as visible any more. Still we were well up on the play. That opportunism gave us five situations (if we count the one that we missed) of which we won three, two of them being blackjacks.

By my calculations, we were up by about five grand by this stage and were getting close to the ceiling that I had placed on our win. I gave the signal to terminate play and Steve and Patty gave me their "confirmed" signals in return. Steve went across and placed another couple of hundred on black on one of the roulette, which also lost but that wasn't a problem, I would rather him do that than not at all.

Steve went to cash in and Patty and I played on at table minimums and a bit above that for about 30 minutes more. We knew exactly where to meet Steve – obviously we couldn't be seen to leave together. Some time later as Patty and I left the casino she asked me how much I thought we had won on the night.

"It's five grand give or take a hundred," I replied.

Patty seemed quite surprised by the accuracy of my answer and asked me if I didn't trust Steve.

"Not at all, Pat, I just like to be thorough that's all. I need to keep a check of these things so I can time our exit," I replied.

That was true though it wasn't the main reason why I was tracking the result, but the answer seemed to satisfy her. After all she was Steve's partner and it was safe to assume that anything that I said to her would get straight back to him. We had only been walking for about ten minutes when we arrived at the spot where Steve had been parked up. I could see as we approached the car that there was someone sitting in the front passenger seat with him.

As I came alongside the car I realised that it was Alex. This was now another person who knew about our operation who didn't need to know. I stooped down to peer through the window slightly, surprising them both. Alex wound the window down and was just about to say something when I said, "Probably not a very good idea to be seen together like this, it's too close to the casino."

They both quickly agreed and Alex got out of the car. Patty and I got in, with me once again getting into the back. About five minutes into the journey home, I asked Steve who Alex was. He gave a very guarded answer that he was a business acquaintance and left it at that.

"You know, Steve, we really cannot have people knowing about our operation like this."

"Oh, he's all right, Carl, trust me."

"But the more people that know, the greater the security risk."

"He's interested in joining us, Carl, and he's prepared to put some money in. What do you think?"

"I don't really know, I will have to give it some thought."

"Anyway, enough about that. We should be celebrating to-night's result."

"How much was it?" asked Patty.

"Four thousand, nine hundred," replied Steve.

That was precisely the figure that I had arrived at. I was pleased with that because it meant that I didn't have to bring up the touchy subject of disagreeing on the amount. If Steve had been out by a couple of hundred, would I have mentioned it? I really don't know the answer to that. Sometimes I wondered who was in charge of the operation because it sure as hell didn't always feel as if I was. Still, at least I had earned myself some money and getting a job could be postponed for just a little while longer. I'll drink to that.

Chapter 14

So, just what is going on?

March 1999

It was fast approaching my birthday, my 31st to be exact, but it was hardly a time for celebration. I don't know what it is about turning 30, it seemed like a pivotal age for me. The passing of my youth into an era of impending middle age. The 20s were gone and so was my youth, or is it this way every time that you reach a landmark age? But that wasn't the only thing that was on my mind; nothing had happened with the blackjack for over two weeks and I was starting to get a little worried. During February and early March we had won just over twenty grand and life couldn't have been sweeter.

But suddenly everything seemed to grind to a halt for no apparent reason. Being the paranoid conspiracy theorist that I am, I was convinced that something was happening behind my back. Were they going it alone without me or was Steve in league with someone else? I knew that Steve had scheduled a trip to the States for March so that would explain why I couldn't reach him, but every time that I called John or Kevin, they seemed to be busy.

I was getting more and more frustrated, and patience was never high on my list of virtues. Kevin had taken a job as a teacher because he had a university degree and John was always into other stuff as well. It was all right for them, but blackjack was all I had at that stage: no blackjack meant no money for Carl. I had the impression that the others were so taken by whether or not we could beat the casinos that it lost its charm once we started doing it.

A bit like the morning after the night you finally get the girl that you have been after for ages into bed – suddenly there is no mystique any more unless you have feelings for her. It wasn't like that for me though. I loved blackjack and it wasn't just the money that motivated me. It couldn't be, because I wasn't earning more than one-sixth of our total winnings anyway. I wasn't earning all that much more than when I was a croupier, but the difference was that I wasn't working anywhere near the same number of hours.

Blackjack was all that I had and no action meant that I was now having to fill my own time more and more. I couldn't sit back and do nothing; there was no point in just using my share of the spoils to be idle for a couple of months. I was earning from the poker game but it wasn't pulling any trees up for me because the stakes were not high enough. In any case, sometimes we only played about once a month anyway.

Richard's visit from London hadn't led anywhere yet, despite him saying that we would be up and running in a couple of weeks. Tony's roulette venture had also been put on the back burner for one reason or another. But my mistake was not only putting all my eggs into one basket, but also putting them all into somebody else's basket. This was my dream and my ambition and I had to do something to kick start it again.

The answer was to have another scouting session, and to play for myself as well. Even if I could manage to take just a couple of hundred off them then it would be great for morale and it would at least get me up off my arse. Yeah, that was it Carl, take the bull by the horns and make something happen. I always knew that something like this would happen either by accident or design and at this stage I wasn't sure which it was.

Surely with twenty-five grand in winnings so far they weren't getting disgruntled? If they were, then these weren't the team members that I had been looking for, but knowing Steve would have tremendous advantages. This was simply because he had introduced me to so many people over the past few weeks, whom I could contact if our team disintegrated. I didn't need Steve; I just needed his money because I still didn't have enough of my own to set up my own team with my own bank-roll. It actually crossed my mind that I may just have to play ball with Steve's desire to hit roulette, although it pains me to say that.

Luckily my expenditure was low and I was very careful with my money during this period. So off I went to go and play solo. Just getting ready to leave the house to drive to the casino was motivation enough for me. After my two week absence from the game, I was back doing what I loved best. Earning just over four grand so far had really fuelled my ambition.

Blackjack had long been my passion but now that I had tasted a little bit of success, it was more obsession than passion. Suddenly the only thing that I wanted to do was to play black-jack; the only thing that I wanted to discuss was blackjack; and the only thing that I wanted to read about was blackjack. I was getting very insular in my outlook and I was fully aware of the dangers of having this type of career. Gambling can be a very addictive pastime, even for anyone who is successful. The win-ners and the losers tend to get addicted for different reasons. I find the intellectually demanding part of it is a massive turn on and I don't mean that in a sexual way (or maybe I do).

So I went on a series of scouting missions to kill the time. All this non activity seemed liked some "phoney war" and it was starting to do my head in. I played five times in three different casinos in the space of two weeks and won about £400 doing nothing in the least bit fancy. This pacified me for a while but the frustration of not playing as a team and earning more money was growing.

I needed to know what was happening because if this continued then I might have had to consider finding a job. The tactics that I was using to earn from blackjack when I was playing on my own were blatant, to say the least, or it certainly seemed that way. There was no excuse now, Steve should be back from Las Vegas and I wanted to know if Kevin was putting teaching before the team.

One evening when I was on my own in the flat, I decided to call Steve. Kevin and John never seemed to have their mobiles turned on and I didn't know where they lived because I had never been to their houses. Patty answered the call almost immediately.

"Hello Pat! It's Carl"

"Oh hello, Carl. How are you? It's been a while." You're telling me I thought, but at least there was enthusiasm in her voice when she realised that it was me. If things were being planned behind my back that didn't involve me, then she may have sounded a little awkward.

"Is Steve there?"

"Yes, I'll just go and get him for you."

I was wondering how to approach the topic of not playing for a while. I knew that Steve or anyone else for that matter certainly didn't owe me a living, but I needed to know where I stood with this thing. The kind of money that we had won so far certainly wouldn't be all that much to Steve – to him it was just some hobby. His business interests were making him far more than that, but it could all be so different if we were to put the time in. After a few moments, Steve came to the phone.

"Hi Carl, I was about to phone you."

Maybe that was true and maybe it wasn't, but we chatted for about ten minutes about various things, with him mainly telling me about his trip to Las Vegas. Finally I asked just what was going on with the blackjack team and I told him that I had not been able to get in touch with John or Kevin. Steve informed me that Kevin was a bit of an oddball character who would quite often go missing, sometimes for months on end.

"Well, that's really not much use to us Steve," I said.

"No, but we don't really need him all that much anyway, do we?" he replied.

He had a point. Kevin was not an ideal team member. He was constantly looking for confrontations and his desire for drink and nightclubbing were not conducive to our interests. Steve informed me that he had been in conversation with Richard that very same day and was looking to start something down south within the next week or so.

This was great news. I would gladly do the travelling if it meant resurrecting my dream. I wasn't an experienced driver and I wasn't too keen on motorway driving having only passing my test the year before, but this would be a great incentive to get the necessary experience. Steve also informed me that Tony would be contacting me shortly after the roulette venture as well.

Suddenly things were starting to look up – maybe I was guilty after all of putting all my faith in a group of people who were less than motivated. At this stage I really needed income from another source; what I had earned from blackjack so far was hardly keeping me in luxury. Steve obviously had numerous other interests and Kevin couldn't be trusted. It was a mistake to assume blindly that everything would go my way and that everyone would drop everything to do exactly what I wanted them to do.

When the conversation with Steve had finished I realised that I didn't have much of a plan; I depended too much on others. Actually, that's not quite true, I just didn't have a plan B. I had prepared this for years but I was naive to think that it would all run like clockwork. Whatever it is in life, you have to work for it and things just don't happen overnight.

I went and made myself a coffee and went up to my room to think and reflect on what we had done so far, what lessons we had learned and more importantly what we needed to do – or should I say what I needed to do. The conversation with Steve had buoyed my confidence but not overly so; I had heard all these promises before. Still though, good news is good news and everything seemed to be back on course, when only a short time ago I had feared the worse. Only time would tell.

CHAPTER 15

BLACK BIRTHDAY

April 1999

The 10 April and it's my birthday. It was about 4pm when I got back from my parents' house. I had to get back in preparation for a blackjack session that evening with the boys and Patty. This was the perfect birthday present for me, everything was back on track (for the time being at least) and my life had focus again. The last few weeks had seemed to go on forever and I was still only really scratching out a living, as I had always done.

The only difference was that I was now working fewer hours and doing something that I loved doing, which seemed a major improvement. Not having the gaming managers telling me what to do and having to put up with their moods and tantrums whenever we were losing was a blessing, and I would do my utmost not to go back to that life again.

We were going to be playing that night back in the same club where I had won playing solo a couple of weeks earlier. I had decided to stay at home and monitor the shuffles on the laptop; gaming staff have very long memories and the sight of me sitting on blackjack would have caused a ripple. Call it stupidity or just desperation to earn a bit of money, but I had jumped from playing close to the table minimum to about three-quarters of the maximum bet on the first box when the trainee dealer pulled one card too many to their own hand and that card was an ace.

I didn't get a blackjack but I won the hand. However, my move was blatant and opportunistic, the kind of thing that croupiers hate because it makes them feel silly. I had done the move before, several times in fact and all in the pursuit of a few quid in the pocket. Hopefully they would just see me as some punk who would eventually lose it all back anyway. But gaming staff do have long memories and for me to go back to the same club when Steve's bets were hitting the felt on the same table would have caused alarm bells.

But I was hoping that they were not going to need me for this trip and even Kevin had decided to grace us with his presence. Anyway, I want to cut straight to the end of the evening because the bottom line was that we lost just under five grand, our first serious reverse. Apparently Steve had refused to go back to the car for the rest of the money and in a later conversation he told me that he didn't trust John and Kevin's ability with the tracking strategies, and that was why he called a halt to the proceedings.

This was some birthday present and suddenly I was back where I started a few weeks ago, with everything on a knife edge again. There had been a massive row in the car going home between Kevin and Steve, with Steve attempting to pull the car across at one stage and drag Kevin out. Kevin had been drinking during the evening and every time that Steve came to the table on their signal, he had lost almost every single hand. In Kevin's defence that is certainly possible even with powerful shuffle tracking strategies and I told Steve this.

With just a few per cent edge at best, losing sessions is inevitable and it may or may not have been their fault. But the point was that Steve had lost confidence in Kevin and John, and I have to say that I can hardly blame him. Although to be fair to John, I believe that if there was anyone responsible for the failure then it was Kevin and me.

I trained him and I briefed him, I also tested Kevin on the tracking strategies so I knew what he could and couldn't do. Maybe I should have been tougher at the beginning and gave Kevin the chop, but I could have been deluding myself by thinking that I had the power to do that anyway. At times it was Steve who seemed to be calling the shots, simply because it was his money, which is a terrible state of affairs to be in.

Steve wanted John and Kevin in from the start because he trusted their knowledge and they were friends. But in my opinion we had come to a point where the entire team was in need of a serious overhaul. I needed to get a grip of the situation and quickly if we were going to succeed. I needed to tell Steve that it may have been his money but he didn't know jack about the game and his constant interfering would seriously undermine our success.

I had been somewhat afraid to speak my mind in the past for fear of being dumped, but the time had come. Losses like this were one thing but to have the financial backer and a team member almost come to blows needs urgent attention. If we were not careful there was a danger that Steve and Patty might go off and do something on their own. In the end Steve was a businessman and he was a very tough one by all accounts. He wasn't going to take losses lightly, especially when people were demonstrating incompetence.

Kevin's past history was working against him and he hadn't helped himself by drinking during a session. Kevin's drinking habits had been a big joke to Steve before, but when his money was on the line it was different. I arranged a meeting at Steve's to try and thrash things out otherwise we were doomed. We were better off not playing at all than carrying on like this.

I arrived at Steve's at about lunch time on the Saturday after my birthday to find him out in the garden watering the flowers. We sat in the garden and talked about flowers and shrubs and stuff, all of which had absolutely no interest for me whatsoever. I just wanted to talk blackjack like I always did. If anyone had asked me what was happening elsewhere in the world I would have struggled to come up with an answer. Anything on blackjack, though, and I wouldn't stop jabbering.

"You know Steve, what happened the other night with Kevin wasn't good."

"He really wound me up, he just wasn't taking it seriously and I was doing my fucking money in," replied Steve.

By the sound of him he was still annoyed so I would have to tread very carefully during this conversation. He had so many other business interests that he could easily just pull the plug on the whole thing.

"You know it may not have been his fault, Steve, these things can happen," I said.

"I can accept the result but getting fucking pissed was his fault though wasn't it? Answer me this and answer it truthfully, do you rate him as a blackjack player – and don't beat about the bush with your answer because I want the truth if I am going to continue."

"In a word...no."

"Why?" asked Steve abruptly.

"Numerous reasons, some you are already aware of and others you are not. He is not the player that you think he is or even that he thinks he is for that matter. He was never successful as a counter simply because he never took the game to a high enough level. He just thought that counting knowledge would get him through and nothing else. Worldwide there are millions like him and casinos love them. I am not knocking his lack of knowledge, what I am knocking is his inability to accept that anyone knows more than him. He has such a massive ego when it comes to blackjack but, if you notice, he seems to be an expert on just about everything."

"Oh believe me, I've noticed."

"John is a totally different character, I can work with John and he will listen but Kevin is impossible to work with at times, and he won't put the time in either," I said.

Steve sat there and listened for a full ten minutes without once interrupting, which was rare for him because he always had something to say. I had his undivided attention now and realised that this was my chance to tell him what I really thought. If I had read the situation right then he would appreciate me for saying what I was about to say.

"There's something else, Steve, and you may not like me saying this, but I think that it needs saying. At the end of the day your money is on the line here, like you said. When you came to me down in Bournemouth, you had the idea of using my expertise to earn money in one capacity or another. Gaming and gambling is all I know and it is all I probably ever will know. What I am trying to say, Steve, is that, well, to be quite blunt...you don't know it."

I went on, "Now before we go any further, I am not saying that you shouldn't have a say in what happens to your own money, I am not saying that at all. It's just that you interfere too often and many of your ideas just don't make any sense. The trouble is that your lack of gaming knowledge means that you don't realise what's right from wrong."

Steve sat there and just stared. I hated it when he did that because you never knew what he was thinking. I continued, "This entire operation has been badly done from the outset in my opinion and another..."

Steve interrupted me for the first time: "Yeah, but we are over twenty grand up so we must be doing something right."

"We are doing some things right, but we are doing an awful lot wrong as well. Firstly you don't do what I tell you to do and neither does Kevin. Secondly, you've told far too many people about what we are doing even if you think that they are OK, and thirdly Kevin and John are not good enough. The only person who seems to be doing exactly what she is told is Patty. Another thing, Steve, you are spending far too much time in the card room."

"So you want Kevin and John out, is that what you are saying?"

"Like I said, I can work with John but Kevin is too much of a loose cannon and, yes, I do think that he should be out. Let's face it, he doesn't turn up half the time anyway and he never put in the practice when I asked him to. This could really go well if we put the time and effort in and adjusted a few things. I know that you have other interests and don't have the time that I have, but if you trust other people with your money then we can still do some damage with this instead of just being ahead a few grand."

"I trust Richard."

"There you go then, at least that's a start."

"He phoned me the other day, by the way, he wants to meet again to sort something out with us."

I smiled and said that I had heard that somewhere before.

"It's true, the last time wasn't a good time for him because he had other things on his mind, but it's different now. He and I have come to an arrangement to play with a joint bankroll, if that's OK by you. We are each putting up half the money so it will help you play without me," said Steve.

"That's great news, but will Patty want to play if you are not there?"

"Oh yeah. I'll be glad to get rid of her for a few hours anyway." Steve smirked in such a way as to indicate that he wasn't joking either.

"Will John go down to London?" I asked.

"I don't know, you will have to ask him but I don't see why not. Mind you, Richard knows a couple of people who can work with us down there so we might not need him. Has Tony called you by the way?"

"No, why have you spoken to him?"

"Yeah, he wants to meet up with you to get this roulette thing sorted and he's prepared to pay you."

I sat upright in my chair for the first time. "How much?" I asked.

"A percentage of what they win but you will have to take it up with Tony. He's a good bloke as well, and if he says that he will pay you then he will," replied Steve.

This was fantastic news; suddenly everything was looking brighter although I had been down that road many times during the past few months. Even if Tony stitched me up for the money then it was still a shot to nothing.

The look of pleasure on my first must have been obvious as Steve said, "Thought that would cheer you up, do you fancy something a bit stronger to drink than a coffee?"

"Why not?" I replied.

CHAPTER 16

THE END OF THE BEGINNING

May 1999

So here we are almost at the end of the book and it is still only 1999. Even though my blackjack adventure (if you can call it that) went on until about 2002, this was almost the end in a way. It was the end of the struggle to get up and running as a professional unit. It was the end of all of the heartache and arguments and indiscipline that had plagued us, at least for the next 18 months.

As I sat with Richard in a bar in west London waiting for the teams to walk out for the champions league final of that year, I couldn't help but feel that the worst was over. Not in the sense that we had cracked it, because you can never assume that in a game like blackjack – it only takes one careless action or casual word and the entire thing blows up in your face.

I was getting sick and tired of all the crap and the hassle, either we did this thing properly or we packed the entire thing in and I did something else. It's surprising how so much shit can wreck a person's dreams and ideals. This wasn't the end but it was the end of the struggle, and I think that makes for a fitting finale to this book.

You will no doubt want to know how we did and I will get to

that in good time. But this book is a story of how blackjack can still be beaten even in the 21st century, even with shuffling machines. It is a story of just why the so-called experts who say that the game is dead as a money maker are wrong, not just in 1998, but even as this book was being written in 2006.

The casinos with their shuffling machines and in house "experts" didn't have a clue what was happening most of the time, although sometimes I felt that they were on to us. Isn't it amazing, just what a divide there is between the north and south of England. As Manchester United and Bayern Munich took the field, a chorus of "We love the Germans" rang out across the bar.

I am not a United fan but I love it when an English club succeeds in European competition, whoever that happens to be. The place erupted when the Germans took an early lead – maybe things are not meant to be for Alex Ferguson's boys in their pursuit of their own holy grail.

My holy grail on the other hand had been reached: the formation of a blackjack team to hit the casinos and hit them hard. It had not worked out entirely as I had planned. In fact hardly anything had gone to plan at all and we had to improvise an awful lot. We added and subtracted personnel along the way at regular intervals and many of them went off and did their own thing once they had been trained.

Even now, I still give coaching to blackjack players in how to beat games with shuffling machines. My meeting with Tony had gone exceptionally well and he had formed his own roulette team, which operated in England and Europe. So how much did we make? Well that is a difficult one to answer simply because so many people were off doing different things during the four years.

From my own personal point of view, I didn't really earn that much. I was earning far more money than when I had been in gaming but when you are working in casinos in the north of England, that wasn't difficult anyway as croupiers were not well paid and couldn't accept tips.

I would say that my expertise and knowledge was responsible for winning an amount that was in the region of a million dollars. I have changed it from pounds to dollars because a million sounds good so please excuse me for that. What we took as a team with Steve and Richard, my own individual sessions, success reported by other blackjack players who I had trained up and Tony's roulette and Caribbean stud poker teams came to around this total.

So the truth is that blackjack never made me rich but it put me into a position where for the first time in my life I had a bit of money behind me. It is the same old story; the real winners are the people with the money and the power. They don't need expertise because money in the right hands just makes even more money. They can buy expertise anywhere and they know that, although in this field, it is harder to find.

Steve and Richard will always make money as will Tony, but people like me seemed forever doomed to grinding it out. But for a short while I was doing something that few people in the entire world have undertaken to do, and I was doing it successfully. The fact that I had done it at all was success in my opinion, even more so because I had once been on the other side of that blackjack table.

I have had successes since. I play professional poker mainly online and succeeding in that field has given me immense satisfaction, though writing and coaching take up a fair amount of my time now so not all my income comes from poker anyway. In fact I am not even sure what the definition of professional actually is. I love what I am doing now but I have never reached the heights of what I felt during that three- to four-year spell of playing blackjack.

That was a high point in my life, a life of constant under-achievement and disappointment was behind me. Blackjack made me feel good about myself and I had not had that sensation in an awful long time. Poker and writing give me satisfaction and a warm glow but blackjack was the buzz that I have failed to recreate since.

Has my life peaked emotionally? I sincerely hope not. On a much bigger scale, I can understand how difficult it must have been for the Apollo astronauts who went to the moon back in the late 1960s and early 70s. They came back and then had to go about living normal lives without ever reaching those highs again. But four years on from the end of it all and there is not an awful lot left now, apart from memories, and that is probably all that should remain. This was my moon landing and my one big step.

Richard was downing drink after drink and wasn't really paying attention to the football; some pretty red head was far more deserving of that. Speaking of Richard, I still see the rest of the boys from time to time and Steve and Patty are still together, which is nice. Kevin is still drifting between teaching and drinking and will never change; John is punting professionally on the betting exchanges. I can't list the names of all of the team members and accomplices in this book for two reasons: it would seem strange when I have not mentioned them before and because there are too many.

But I hope that if ever they are reading this book they will recognise some of the events of that period and smile, just as I look back and smile now. I would like to take this opportunity once again to thank you all for giving me something that I have never had before in my life...excitement and purpose. I would also like to thank you for your discretion along the way because if it hadn't been for this then our "career" wouldn't have lasted the time that it did.

Someone famous once said "perseverance can achieve any-thing", I think that it was John D. Rockefeller although I apolo-gise profusely if it was someone else. This is true: just ask any-one who was watching the football that evening who witnessed Manchester United score twice in injury time to win the Cham-pions League. When the second goal went in and I knew that the Germans barely had time to kick off, I leapt from my chair screaming and shouting. It just goes to show you…dreams can come true!